Geometrical Patterns *of* Ancient Icons

GEOMETRICAL PATTERNS OF ANCIENT ICONS

DR. A.P. SINGH

AGAM

AGAM KALA PRAKASHAN

DELHI - 110 052

First Published 2010

ISBN : 978 -81-7320-098-4

Published by:
Dr. Agam Prasad, M.A., Ph.D., Diploma in Museology
For **Agam Kala Prakashan**
34, Central Market, Ashok Vihar
Delhi - 110 052
Tel.: 27212195, 47098550, 65688806-7
Fax: 91-11-27212195
Email: agambooks@gmail.com, agambook@yahoo.com
www.agamkala.com

Composed by:
Aman Printographics
Delhi - 110 052
Mobile: 9891395309

Printed by:
Chawla Offset
Delhi-110 052

Printed in India

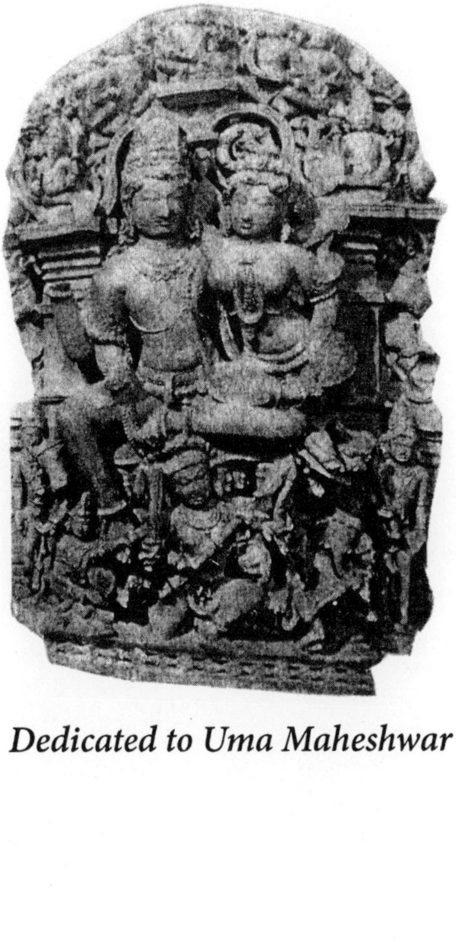

Dedicated to Uma Maheshwar

CONTENTS

Preface 9

List of illustrations 11

Chapter 1:

Stage of Human Evolution, Anatomical Features and Geometrical Patterns of Torso of Icons of different Sects of Ancient India 17

Chapter 2:

Ancient Icons Iconographical Features of Ancient Icons Under Different Trends of India 25

Chapter 3:

Icon Worship, Tantriccult and Tantric Centres of Ancient India 67

Chapter 4:

Hand Poses, Ornaments, Drapery Asanas, Standing, Sitting, Sayana, Dancing and Bhanga, Postures of Ancient Icons 85

Chapter 5:

Conclusion 91

Select Bibliography 97

Index 103

Figures 109

Plates 117

PREFACE

The present critical study of geometrical patterns of Icons of different sects of various dynasties of ancient India, is an humble attempt being contemplated by me for the first time.

It is beyond my sacred and pleasant task to acknowledge the help I received in the execution of this book.

Shri Shiv Pal Singh my eldest son, carried out the photography of Icons and other objects The layout was prepared by Dr. Harpal Singh my yonger son, Dr. Apurva D. Yadav and Akriti Yadav and Dr. Bhuvan Singh also were helpful to me. I thank them.

I am extremely thankful to Dr. Rahman Ali Rtd. Prof. of Ancient Indian History and Culture Vikram University, Ujjain who was very helpful to me in the preparation of this book.

Like wise Shri P.J. Abraham, Dy. Director Technical of Directorate of Archaeology and Museums helped me in various ways, I thank him.

It is beyond expression to account for the encouragement given by my beloved wife Smt. Meena Devi and my daughter in laws Smt. Priya lata and Dr. Puja Singh due to which I could undertake this work inspite of preoccupations with family.

Apart from the above mentioned scholars and well wishers I record my sincere gratitude to all those whose names are not mentioned but helped me in various ways to complete this work.

I am also thankful to Dr. Agam Prasad and Staff of Agam Kala Prakasan for publishing the book in such a short period.

28th Jan 2010

Dr. A.P. Singh
25, A Sector
Sarvadharma Colony
Kohar Road
Bhopal - 462016

LIST OF ILLUSTRATIONS

FIGURES

Fig. 1 Various stages of Human evolution.

Fig. 2 Javaman, Pekingman, Neanderthalman, and Cromagnonman.

Fig. 3 Geometrical patterns of Ancient Icons (Torso) Indus valley civilization 3rd - 4th Millennia, B.C.

- A. Dancing girl from Harappa
- B. Kuber yaksa from Besnagar (Vidisha)
- C. Yaksi from Ahichhatra (Allahabad)

Fig. 4 Satvahana period/1st century B.C./1st century A.D.

- A. Depiction of parabola pattern of Torso in images of Toran gate of Sanchi
- B. Depiction of parabola pattern in image of Gandhara style of Buddha. Stupa Kusana period 2nd century A.D.
- C. Depiction of Hyperbola pattern in image of Gupta period.

Fig. 5 Kalcuri period 6th century A.D. 11th century A.D.
A. Depiction of Hyperbola pattern in images of Kalcuri period.
B. Dipiction of Bi-triangular pattern in the images of pratihara period 8th century A.D. - 10th century A.D.
C. Depiction of Bi-Triangular pattern in image of Parmara period 10th century A.D. - 12th century A.D.

Fig. 6 A. Depiction of trapezoid pattern of images of candella period 10th century A.D. - 12th century A.D.
B. Depiction of trapezoid pattern in images of Kachhapaghata period 10th century A.D. - 12th century A.D.

Fig. 7 Hand poses of different Icons.

Fig. 8 Hand poses (Mudras) of different Icons.

PLATES

Pl. 1 A. Dancing girl of Indus valley.
B. Icon of Priest of Indus valley.

Pl. 2 Kuber yaksa from Besnagar Vidisha 2nd century B.C.

Pl. 3 Yaksi from Ahichhatra (Allahabad) Sunga period.

Pl. 4 Kuber Yaksa from Badoh, Vidisha 7-8th century A.D.

Pl. 5 A. Chamar dharini yaksi, Sunga period
B. Yaksi of Sunga period representing ornaments and drapery.

Pl. 6 Buddha Standing Kushana Period Gandhar Style

Pl. 7 A. Dhyansta Buddha in asana (Seated) Kushana period, Gandhara Style.

B. Budha seated in padmasana, preaching- Mudra, Kushana period, Mathura Style.

Pl. 8 Buddha seated in padmasana from swatvally Afghanistan Kushana period, Gandara style.

Pl. 9 Kumar Kartikeya, Gajendra Ghat, Mandsaur 4th - 5th century A.D.

Pl. 10. Kaumari, Nachand, Panna 6th century A.D.

Pl. 11. Siva Parvati, Ramvan Museum, Satna 5th- 6th century A.D.

Pl. 12. Maheshwari, Nanchand, Panna 6th century A.D.

Pl. 13 Vaishnavi, Nanchand, Panna 6th century A.D.

Pl. 14 Indrani, Nanchand, Panna

Pl. 15 Divilingi Lakulisha, Gajendra ghat, Mandsaur 4th- 5th century A.D.

Pl. 16 Siva Lakulisha, Satna, 5th century A.D.

Pl. 17 Lakuhsha in Padmasana Hinglajgarh, Mandsaur 8th century A.D.

Pl. 18 Indrani, Kota, Shivpuri 7th - 8th century A.D.

Pl. 19 Kamdeva, Vidisha region, Vidisha 8th century A.D.

Pl. 20 Natesh Siva (Bhikshatan Murti) Hinglajgarh, Mandsaur 8th century A.D.

Pl. 21 Uma-Maheswara, Indragarh, Mandsaur 8th century A.D.

Pl. 22 Ganesh, Keldhar, Shivpuri 8th century A.D.

Pl. 23 Shalbhanjika, Gyaraspur, Vidisha 9th - 10th century A.D.

Pl. 24 Hari- Hara, Shivpuri (Region) Shivpuri 9th - 10th century A.D.

Pl. 25 Uma - Maheswara (Ravananugrha Murti), Hinglajgarh, Mandsaur 11th century A.D.

Pl. 26 Abhisarika, Hinglajgarh, Mandsaur 11th century A.D.

Pl. 27 Gauri, Hinglajgarh, Mandsaur 11th century A.D.

Pl. 28 Visnu (Newly Discovered) Sunari Village, Vidisha 11th century A.D.

Pl. 29 Uma-Maheswara, Hinglajgarh Mandsaur 11th century A.D.

Pl. 30 Shakti Ganesh, Mandsaur 11th century A.D.

Pl. 31 Parvati, Bhanpura, Mandsaur 11th century A.D.

Pl. 32 Hari Hara (Seated in Ardha Padmasana) Hinglajgarh, Mandsaur 11th century A.D.

Pl. 33 Uma- Maheswara, Hinglajgarh Mandsaur 11th century A.D.

Pl. 34 Uma-Maheswara, Barhad, Bhind 11th century A.D.

Pl. 35 Kartekeya (Sthanak Murti) Hinglajgarh, Mandsaur 11th century A.D.

Pl. 36 Hari- Hara (Sthanak Murti) Hinglalgarh, Mandsaur 11th century A.D.

Pl. 37 Visnu, Vidisha 12th century A.D.

Pl. 38 Jain Chatustika Phulpur, Vidisha 12th century A.D.

Pl. 39 Tri-deva, Mankhedi, Jabalpur 10th century A.D.

Pl. 40 Uma Maheswara, Jabalpur 10th century A.D.

Pl. 41 Vaisnavi, Dhubela, Chhatarpur 11th century A.D.

Pl. 42 Vaman, Semaria, Shahdol 11th century A.D.

Pl. 43 Krisna- Janma, Shahdol 11th century A.D.

Pl. 44 Yogini Shahdol 12th century A.D.

Pl. 45 Skhalit Vasna, Jabalpur Museum, Jabalpur 13th century A.D.

Pl. 46 Siva (Sambhanga) Darpan naika and erotic image (Mithuna Pratima) Khajuraho (Chhatarpur) 10 - 11th century A.D.

Pl. 47 Apsara, Khajuraho 10 - 11th century A.D.

Pl. 48 Apsara, Khajuraho 11th - 12th century A.D.

Pl. 49 Avlokites'wara, Mausania, Chhatarpur 10th century A.D.

Pl. 50 Siva Barhad, Bhind 11th century A.D.

Pl. 51 Adinath Narwar, Shivpuri 12th century A.D.

Pl. 52 Vaisnavi, Shivpuri 11 - 12th century A.D.

Pl. 53 Ambika, Shivpuri 11th - 12th century A.D.

Pl. 54 Visnu, Vishvarupa, Suhania, Morena 10th century A.D.

Pl. 55 Alas Naika Morena 10th century A.D.

Pl. 56 Buddha (Seated in Padmasana) (Bhumisparsa Mudra) Keldhar, Shivpuri 10th century A.D.

1

STAGE OF HUMAN EVOLUTION, ANATOMICAL FEATURES AND GEOMETRICAL PATTERNS OF TORSO OF ICONS OF DIFFERENT SECTS OF ANCIENT INDIA

Since the dawn of human evolution on this earth crust, the ape man's civilization was spotted by the cultural remains of ancient times.

This may be marked as the beginning of new era for the sequential evolution of man in stages[1].

This Civilization of man limited to dense forests who started his home land making over the shaddy groves of trees, over the thick branches of tall trees, living on vegetal food. Later on when the cranial capacity increases to maximum of cromagnon 1650 cc. and 1300 to 1600 c.c. of homocepian man.

Prehistoric man

Habilis man was the first inventrr of tool making. They lived in caves, by nature they were omnivorous and also show cannibalism i.e.,

[1] Fig-1 various stages of human evolution.

at the time of paucity of food for them in the forest then they eat the flesh of members of their own species too. It includes Java man, peking man, Heidel berg man.

In human evolution only the Neanderthal man lived in the huts prepared by him, rest of species lived in caves.

The following are the characteristic features of the prehistoric man[1].

1. **Homo Habilis.**

   Cranial Capacity

   650-800 Cubic Centimeter

   Volume in which brain is kept

   Jaw U shaped

   Position of head on vertebral

   Column - progna thous, i.e.

   head is protuding out from the

   vertical column, Erect posture

   Chin absent.

2. **Homo Erectus (Direct ancestors of Homosapiens.**

   (a) **Javaman (Erect ape man)**

   first man who used fire for

   hunting, protection and cooking

   Cranial capacity - 800-1000 c.c.

   Jaw U shaped

   Position of head on vertical column

[1] Fig- 2- Java man Peking man, Neanderthal man, Cromagnon man.

Prognathus

Erect Posture

Chin obsent

(b) Peking man

They used sharp Chisel Shaped
tools of stones, bones for cutting
and killing animals

Cranial Capacity - 850 - 1300 c.c.

Jaw U shaped, position of head

On vertebral column - prognan thus

Erect position

Chin absent.

(c) Heidelberg man

Cranial capacity - 1300 c.c.

It is believed that this species was evolved as a branch from main line of evolution and got extinct after sometimes

3. Homosapiens

(a) Neanderthal man

Origin and evolution before 40,000-1 lakh year cranial Capacity - 1300 -1600 c.c.

(Same as Homosapiens, seipien or Modern man.

Jaw semicircular

Position of Head on vertical column orthognathus

Erect position

Less developed chin

(b) Cromagnon man.

Origin and evolution - 10,000-50,000 years ago

Cranial Capacity - 1650 c.c. (Maximum)

Erect Posture.

Well developed chim.

Semicircular Jaw.

Position of head on vertical column- orthognathous Domestication of animal started bythem. Larger fore head, well developed speach centre.

(c) Homo - sapiens (Modern man)

Man of today

Cranial Capacity 1300-1600 c.c.

(Same as Neanderthal Man)

Origin and evolution - 10000 - 11000 years ago.

Jaw - semicircular, position head on vertical column - orthognathous, well developed chin and speach centre, smaller fore head.

(d) Homo sapiens futuralies

after Homosapiens sapiens, the man of further species will have hairless body taller, tomb like head and larger brain , palm with no fifth finger.

Anatomical Features

The human body is divided into head neck torso (trunk), and limbs. The trunk is subdivided into chest or thorax and belly or abdomen.

In standing posture, it is called "Sama bhanga" posture, an upright position, the upper limbs hanging by the sides and the palms of the hands directed forwards. This is the anatomical position.

Superior or Cephalic (towards the head) therefore refers to the position of a part that is nearer to the head of a supposedly up right body, while inferior means nearer the feet. Caudal (towards the tail) can replace inferior in the trunk (torso).

The median plane is an imaginary plane, i.e., X-axis That olivides the body into two apparently equal halves, right and left and Y-axis into upper and lower halves.

The anterior and posterior median lines are the edges of the plane on the front and back of the body.

So far as the ancient icons are concerned these have been fashioned by the skilled artisans under various royal patronage, the edges of plane of torso is confirmed into various geometrical patterns, discussed in forth coming pages likewise the rotational features in dancing postures of icons, where all movements take place at joints and may occur in any plane.

The movements of the torso in the segital plane are known as flexion (bending interiorly) and extension (straightening or bending posteriorly).

It is to point out here that the limbs, flexion is applied to the movement which carries the limb anteriorly and folds it., extension to the movement which carries it posteriorly and straightens it. At the ankle, confusion is avoided by the use of the terms plantar flexion (Movement towards the sole) and dorsiflexion (Movement towards the dorsum)

Movement of the Torso in the coronal plane are known as lateral flexion. While in the limbs they are called abduction (movement away from the median plane. At the wrist abduction (radial deviation) refers to the movement of the hand towards the ulnar (little finger side.) In the fingers, and toes, abduction means the spreading apart and adduction the drawing together of degits in the plane of the finger or toe nails. In the hands this movement is away from or towards the line of second toe.

The thumb lies in the plane at right angles to that of the fingers. Hence abduction, respectively, carry the thumb anteriorly and posteriorly.

The dance performance by divine dancers Sanchi Stupa-1 and dance performance at Deogarh (5th Century A.D. - 7th Century A.D.), Aurangabad Cave VII) are rare representation of rhythemic movement of body and soul coupled together.

So far as the postures of the dance performance is concerned by the maidens (Central figure) Aurangabad cave no. VII the shape of the legs appears to be diamond design in geometrical pattern is a specific representation, depict female theatrical troupes.

The above dance scene is alike that of the dance scene that has been painted in Ajanta cave no. 1.

The dance scene performances by maidens even in Buddhist temple appears to have been in vogue in that period possibly due to the Mahayan influence.

This fact is authenticated to the depiction of dance scene in cave no. VII. The representation of Geometrical diamond pattern of the legs in the dance scene of Deograh (5th Century A.D.) in worth mention over here.

Icons of different sects

From the close study of ancient icons of different sects, those in situ, and displayed and preserved in various museums have been brought together. A comprehensive photography has been done and icons, and problems have been critically discussed in the present text.

Further it is analysed that the artisans (Silpis) followed the norms of the carving icons with the application of geometrical patterns at various stages of development of faith. It appears that worshiping the gods in Human forms become prevalent from few centuries before Christian era.

Since the days of evolution of folk art during yaksa cult these are the indigenous experiment of the local artisans based on the artistic endevours under sungas satvahnas to classical Guptas and subsequent changes and continuities in fashioning of the icons in geometrical forms and decoration under the Pratiharas, Kalcuris, Parmaras, Chandellas and Kachhapaghatas as the feadul society with its individual distinctive social codes and behavioral styles developed, its Idioms and norms.

It is to point out here that specifically the icons of Siva through history with the growing fusion of contemplative fervour and physical vehemence, can probaly be seen in strzygowskian terms as the result of the dialogue of the northern, geometrical, symbolical, non-naturalistic art, with the southern naturalistic art of the line, with volume. Coomasaswamy would call this process, a product, not superficial blend of styles but of a crossing of fundamental spiritual tendencies.

In the present context, an attempt has been made to examine critically the genesis and development of art style particularly the geometrical patterns of torso of icons.

In the preceding pages anatomical features of human body has been discussed briefly along with the evolution of man at various stage of the development and characteristic features of man.

It is noteworthy that for the first time an attempt has been made to study the geometrical pattern of icons. The interpretations have been authenticated by a number of illustrations sect wise and the charts and figures.

Thus the contribution of silpis and dynasties of the particular regions of India as a whole have been assessed. It is expected that the present contribution of the author will help the scholars and common mass to understand different trends of icons as a whole.

However the following geometrical patterns of "Torso" of different sects are given below for our reference.

Indus civilization	cylindrical pattern	Fig. 3
Yaksa cult	Rectangulars pattern	
Sunga period	Parabola, pattern	
Satvahana peiod	Parabola, pattern	Fig. 4
Kushana period	Parabola pattern	
Gupta period	Hyperbola, pattern	
Kalcuri period	Hyperbola, pattern	Fig. 5
Pratihāra period	Bi-triangular, pattern	
Parmāra period	Bi-triangular, pattern	
Candella period	Trapezoid pattern	Fig. 6
Kachhapa ghata period	Trapazoid pattern	

2

ANCIENT ICONS
ICONOGRAPHICAL FEATURES OF ANCIENT ICONS UNDER DIFFERENT TRENDS OF INDIA

The term Icon (derived from Greek ekion) signifies and objects of worship. The English word Image derived from old French and Latin "Imago" basic cannotation of likness. The words like pratikriti, Pratima, Vimba means reflection. The sense of the image of divinities.

Like wise, the term Icon represents, a figure, image, a portrait carved in stone in low, high or bold relief However it is to point out here that various of artists like sutradhara, sthapati, silpi and Rupkara were employed by the ruler of various dynasties for the development of art and Iconography.

In the early Indian art the wood and elay were two cheep media for fashioning, carving of Icons. Later on bone, Ivory, stone and metal were utilised for preparing images by the silpis.

The word "Sila" or "Saila" was used for stone work to distinguish it from the other media. Icons of different sects were mostly prepared from the lithic media than in other media.

The art is for art's sake and art was an attractive and impressive medium for the development of religion, it was utilized by various faiths. It is because of this region, there was a great demand of skilled silpis for preparing the Icons in different parts of the country.

The artists were required to be conversant not only with aesthetics but also with the emotional thought, socio-religious trend of their times.

It is to point out here that some of the Buddhist and Jaina monks were expert artists and carved out excellent images, both in the plastic or pictorial art.

Some of the images figures were made at various art centres like, Mathura, Sarnath, Ajanta and Bagh which were prepared by the monks artists. Mention may be made of the monk yasadinna who prepared two stone images of Buddha at Mathura during the reign of Kumargupta I. these two representative images are excellent at par and representative excellent work monship of Gupta period.

It is to mention over here that good artist "silpis" or "Sailopakaras" by the rulers to far off places to carve out good images of deities at those places.

Ancient Indian iconography occupies a prominent place in the history of arts. The rich and varied forms viz Geometrical patterns Which developed in this country during a long span of time are remarkable from the points of view of antiquity, quality and quantity.

The efflorescence of plastic art that exhibited in the Indus vally culture during the 3rd millennia B.C. and 4th millenia B.C. is a path finder in the history of art of India as seen in the centres at Harappa and Mohen-Jodaro. Its remains have been discovered from Punjab in the North to southern parts of Gujarat and from Sind to Meerut, Saharanpur district of Uttar Pradesh in the cast.

The art of this civilization was essentially secular in character. The religious ingredients in some form, however, began to appear in that art.

The Vedic culture borrowed and later assimilated, several elements of the Indus civilization viz symbolism of that art which became a source material for different art culture of India during the proto historic and historic periods respectively, was to some extent inspired by the symbology of Indus valley art. Icons like dancing girl nude (Nigroface) from Harappa Method of preparation was applique one[1] and priest[2] are unique findings.

The Vedic pantheon in course of time, gave rise to various religious forms, the chief being vaisnavism, saivism and saktism, Vishnu, Siva and Sakti (Goddess) were the main deities of devotion apart from the Ganpati, surya were another centres of worship.

From 6th century B.C. Buddhism and Jainism grew up and developed into two major Indian religions.

One of the chief media of propogation was utilized in the form of fine arts. These included the icons of different sects, paintings and performing arts like music, dance and drama.

In ancient India religion is the main cause of life. The "Dharma" in the broad sense implied the ideas of mortality and righteousness.

In the ritualistic sense it enjoyed the norms and details of worshipping the deities in shrines.

There was a strong idea of emotional integration through out the country and one broad assimilative culture among the inhabitants of this great land.

---

[1] Plate - 1 (A)

[2] Plate - 1 (B)

Followers of various religions were happy in their own rituals and ceremonies without quarrelling against the followers of other religions. This was possible due to the concept of one country and one broad assimilative culture among the inhabitants.

In ancient India the modern idea of "art for art sake" had not taken any roots. Art had a wider connotation. It was deeply associated with religion in its broad sence and was regarded as an integral part of culture. There are strong evidences to show that the followers of the Vedic, Puranic pantheons, the Buddhists the Jains and others lived peacefully side by side in the towns and villagers the examples of ancient towns of Mathura, Vidisha, Pataliputra, Vaisali, Malhar, Badami, Varanasi etc. Can be sited in this respect.

So far as the worship of deities are concerned, it is to mention over here that some inscriptions contain interesting "Dhyanas" to various deities. These dhyanas are helpful in determining the Iconographic forms of gods and goddesses and their correct designations. For examples Siva is mentioned in the inscriptions as Pasupati, Mahesvara, Lakulisa, umapati, Kalyan sundera or ardhnarishvara.

Like wise Vishnu is contemplated as Vasudeo, Janardan, Narayana, Murari, Sripati etc.

The two words "Bodhisattava and Buddha is also mentioned as sakyamuni, pitamah, and samyak-sambhudda on some early rcords there and other such terms provide us a glimps of recognition or identifying the images and knowing the exact iconographic forms of the deities. The synthetic trends in Indian religions are also known from the syncretic ancient icons discovered in large numbers throughout the country. The cult images also indicate the fusion of two important elements in Indian religion and art viz; "Yoga" (meditation) and "Bhoga" (pleasure).

So for as the Iconography is concerned, it deals with the Icons. Basic concept of Icons is that they were made with the basic aim of being worshiped with devotional sentiment, (The Bhakti). The real devotion provides the submission to the lord before whose Icons a devotee concentrates himself. Apart from the cult images and others meant for the subsidiary deities and semi-Devine and decorative figures, ancient Indian art has an important element viz; the symbolic representation. In this context we may mention the Hinyana sect of Buddhist art at Sanchi Stupa, we have got the symbolic representation carved on the Toranas of four gate ways an aniconic form of representation.

The significance of the art symbols cannot be minimized. several symbols are known in some archaic rock paintings also, eg. the symbols of sun, the moon and the fire. These are a few other symbol also occur on coins, seals and sealings.

At the initial stage these symbols are shown in the natural forms of the sun, moon fire etc. later on they assume human form as seen in the Icons of different sects of Indian art.

Besides Surya several other Vedic Puranic deities are represented on the coins of panchala rulers and also on the coins of Satvahanas, the Kshatrapas, the Kushanas, the Yaudheyas, the Kunindas, the Guptas etc.

Besides the religious and secular symbols, the figures of animals and birds also occur on coins seals and sealings.

If we compare the portryal of the figures of Siva on coins of Kushanas with that found on the coins of Yaudheyas, we can find one similarity.

The contemporary coins of yaudheyas bear almost the same traits (feature of torso) and facial expressions in the depiction of Siva as we find on kushana coins.

The epigraphic records of Kushana period discovered from Eastern Malwa refer to the name of Vaskusena dated year 22 (100 A.D.) and also the image of Vasiska year 28 (106 A.D.) at Sanchi (District Raisen) Substentiate the influence of Kushana over central India[1], where images of Buddha were made from Mathura School of art.

Iconographical features of Ancient Icons under different trends of India

In preceding pages an attempt has been made to examine the genesis and development of art, Icons, beginning with the 3rd and 4th Milenia B.C.

In the broad sence the worship is associated with the Icons, while Iconography deals with the Icons where as Icons were made with the basic aim of being worshiped.

The main cause of worship is the devotional sentiment (Bhakti) in Indian language.

The word Iconography is derived from the Graphic, the art of illustration, the study, description, cataloging or collective representation of portrait under different trends of art.

A real devotion is a submission to It's (god) before whose icon a devotee concentrates himself.

The basic concept of "Bhakti" is complete surrender (Samaspana) before the "Lord". It provides the devotee the sense of salvation and devotion (Bhavna) and Samarpana are the two coeval form which inculcate deep feeling for worship of deity of this inner feeling is not generated, the worship will be aimless and superficial, as worship is an outcome of devotional sentiment rooted deeply in Bhakti.

---

[1] Marshall J. Catalogue of the Museums of Archaeology at Sanchi, 1922, P-30.

In a word, Indian "art, and crafts" in their crudent and noblest forms, have their moorings in a concept of Dharma or an obsolute, pervasive moral order. A riot of carnal images on the external facade of the temple yields place to contemplative silence in the cavernous depth of the sanctum sanctorum. All the pomp and display of military out works or vain places vying with sky, surround, in their midst, quiet humble shrines. Life at one place, is depicted in its acquisitive frenzies and the purple flow of physical enjoyment. Hugging close to this lurid life and overshadowing it, there are pictures of oblivious self absorption, and complete renunciation.

It is as if all the sound and fury all the battles and exertions are but for reaching the unruffled calm of a sea of inner consciousness.

Enjoyment here is almost a gateway to renunciation.

Yaksa Cult

The icons of yaksa were fashioned carved round under folk art by the local artisans as an indegenous effort by them, without any patronage of Royal dynasty.

The yaksa images fasioned in bold relief, they are robust and gigantic, free standing images have been discovered from a large part of India, located in out skirt of the villages. These images have been found located in Kurushetra to orissa, Ahichhatra to Vidisha and magadha to surparaka. From this it appears that the popularity of Yaksa cult was well established.

Yaksa is generally noted by the villagers as "Gaon, gaon Ko veer, Gaon gaon ko siddha".

He is brave and protects village to village and who has attained the power of salvation for village to village.

He is worshiped by the villagers as "Jakhaiya baba". Villagers have great faith in Yaksa and believe that during an epidemic in the village, the Jakhaiya baba will restore the villagers from panic to peace, by their prayers.

This prayer is performed in group of people to the village lead by an old experienced man, who moves forward holding a fresh earthen pot full of water, while other follow him in a chain.

The leader sprinkles drop of water all around the village chanting hymns in favour of Yaksa and the epidemic disease is gone.

Yaksa cult was prevalent prior to the Mauryan times. From artistic point of view, the scholars have ascribed the date of Icons of Yaksa to a period ranging from 4th century B.C. to circa 2nd century B.C.

It in interesting to point out here that a detailed study of Yaksa and Yaksi images have been done by Dr. promod chandra is a note worthy fact.[1]

It is to point out again here that in the year 1952, Betwa river (District Vidisha) over flooded cutting the side bands of Benagar. creating great huvock for the villages.

It is after receding the flood, people of Besnagar saw a numbers of images lying in the bed of river and discovered a gigantic image of kuber Yaksa belonging to 2nd century B.c. lying down ward and the people started washing clothes over the back to the image.

---

[1] Promod chandra - Yaksa and Yaksi statues from Besnagar art. Orientals vol VII 1996, P- 157-63.

Primarily it was shifted to the compound to P.W.D. rest house of Vidisha, later on when the building of Archaeological Museum Vidisha was constructed, this image was displayed there.

The right hand of the image is missing. His turbon is twisted to the left whose knot is of the usual fashion used in Sunga period. Physiological point of view his face is oval shaped, the Torso is rectangular.

The expression of face is like a westler's face, He holds a vasni (Purse) full of coins, a symbol of wealthy man, on account of this insignia the yaksa is recognized as Kuber yaksa the god of welth.[1]

It is to mention over here that a good number of yaksa and yaksi images have been discovered from Besnagar belonging to 1st century B.C. to 3rd century A.D.

One of the yaksi image from Besnagar belonging to circa Ist century A.D. is displayed in Calcutta Museum.

From the above finding of yaksa image in Besnagar from 2nd century B.c. we may conclude that this area became the production centre of yaksa images by the local artisans using the sedimentary rock of sand stone, locally easily available in abundance, suitable for fashioning the yaksa images and this trend continued till 4th - 5th century A.D. in this region.

Like wise a terracotta image of yaksi belonging to Sunga period was recovered from an archaeological excavation at Kausambi (District Allahabad)[2].The yaksi is standing in "Sambhanga" posture. On the head is a big knot as usual fashion of Sunga period however this tradition is still prevelent in Rajasthan.

---

[1] Plate - 2.

[2] Plate - 3.

Face is ovalshaped bearing a thick neckless ornament. Torso of the image is parabolic.

It is to point out here that a life size image of yaksi belonging to Sunga period is enshrined over a high platform by the local people of village Bhatanvara (District Satna), witnessing remarkable features and is under worship there.

The people of this village have great faith on this living image, who are of the opinion that this yaksi is protecting the village from all calamities, as it was believed in the yaksa cult.

It may also be mentioned that according to "Atharveda" Kuber is designated "Yaksa-Raj" It is mentioned in Ramayana that Kuber is the "Manas Putra" of Brahma, who appointed him as guard of treasure of Gods and that is why he called "Dhanapati" At a certain occasion is seen flying the puspaka viman, made by Vishwakarma.

It is to mention over here that an image of Kuber[1] belonging to 7-8th century A.D. is explored in the midst of the forest of Badoh (District-Vidisha) is a rare image of its own kind. The image is seated on high seat, one of whose feet is resting over pots of welth indicating him as the guard of this welth. He is holding a purse of coins in one of his hand. Lotus hallow is seen in the back of face. on either side of kuber is seen a yaksi holding chamar serving him.

It is to point out here that load bearing yaksa as (kichaka) are represented in temples below the beams under various dynasties.

It is again to point out here that a lofty image locally called "Ravan Tol" is still lying near the village Ravan is an unique gigentic image of Siva belonging to Parmar period. Rgveda accounts at various stages about the worship of Kuber. Kuber is enshrined over a lofty platform

1 Plate - 4.

with out any roofing in sama bhang posture in the out skirt of the village, the site where it is located is known as Brahmapuri and is also named "Aprajita".

Apart from the yaksa kuber at Archological Museum at Vidisha. There are three more images viz. parkham yaksa at parkham village (District Mathura), the third one is recovered from patna and the fourth kuber image of yaksi is worshiped in a temple at Madurai, which is Goddess Meenakshi, the daughter of Kuber all in standing posture.

It is however to point of here that the circa 2nd century B.C. was on its high esteem of yaksa cult and a peak period of popularity in Vidisha region, due to which there was a large demand for production of these images by artisans, and this lasted upto 7th-8th century A.D. in Dasarna region as is authenticated by an seated image found in Badoh (District Vidisha).

Like wise from padam pawaya or padmavati we have the yaksa and yaksinis. The pot bellied yaksa, datable to 3rd century A.D. is manibhadra wearing the cobra and sacred thread and acting as "Nagara-devata" or the presiding deity of the village keeping disease at bay.

A glance at the yaksa images from parkham (Mathura Museum) Patna, yaksa (Indian museum) shows how the tundila (pot bellied) trait of yaksas was incorporated in a much later text utilised by Hemadari.[1]

[1] Chandra- R.P. Article on four yaksa statues in J.D.L. Vol. IV (1921) PP 47-84.

Salbhanjikas - Nayikas, Abhisarikas, Sursundaries (Apraras)

As regards the images of Salbhanjikas Nayakas, Abhisarikas, Sursundaries, we have noticed them at different hooks and nooks of Madhya Pradesh region viz; the temples of Pratihara, Kalcluris, Candellas etc.

The well know salbhanjika motif occuring profusely in Indian art and literature was the gradual out come of the historical background.

The sankrit term Salbhanjika is equivelent to the pali term "Salbhanjiya" which initially signified the form of udyankrida (a part time play of ladies in the Garden)[1].

Panini, in his Astadhyayi has mentioned Salbhanjika as a favourite sport of eastern people (pragdesavartti-namakrida)[2].

Vatsyayan has also indicated his familiarity with Salbhanjika (i.e. bending the branch of mango tree) as a popular game of the ladies[3].

Mention may be made particularly during Maurya and Sunga Satvahana period the Salbhanjika motif was fully evolved and it was profusely carved out on the brackets of Buddhist toranas and railing pillars of stupas. The popular depictions of Salbhanjikas in the art of Sanchi, Mathura, Amaravati and Nagarjunakonda deserve special mention.

The form of Salbhanjika denoted two district seenes of Indian art first was purely auspicious and related with the nativity seenes of Buddha. While the second type was the form of non-nativity which

---

[1] Rao . T.A.G. Elements of Hindu Iconography Travencore- 193, Vol.II P5/5.

[2] Rao. U.N. Salbhanjika in art philosphy and literature Allahabad 1979, P.1.

[3] Ibid.

was more fairly popular and figured prominently as lovely art motif usually represented by charming beauty scanty dressed or semi nude but adorned with a broad girdle partly covering her nakedness etc.

Likewise the Abhisarikas are:

(1) Diwabhisarika	-	Paribhoga- darsika, the day light lover with appreciative monkey looking up wards and some times pulling down the sari of the Abhisarika.
(2) Nisabhisarika	-	Moving in the darknight to meet the lover.
(3) Jyotsna-Abhisarika	-	Shrinking shyly against her lover.
(4) Raksa bhisarikar or	-	The nocturnal lover edging close to the by of her lover in fearless and complete surrender.

Likewise the Various Nayikas

(1) Darpana Dharini Nayika	-	Holding a mirror.
(2) Praudha Nayika	-	Holding a child in her lap
(3) Vasak-sajja Nayika	-	Holding a box of cosmetics
(4) Anjana- Nayika	-	Applying anjana in her eye
(5) Manini - Nayika	-	Who is a huff and being persuaded by her lover to relent in the garden beneath the bower.

(6) Apsara Nayika[1]

(7) Alas Nayika

Above all, there are the Nayikas and Sursundaris from Suhania, who are holding lamps or who have just taken bath, their body glistening with dripping water, flexing their limbs or shaking their hair dry, over a vision of naked loveliness.

Most intriguing is the lady, who has tied a bell to her girdle on her slim waist, obviously tied there by her husband as an alarm bell to signal her untoward movements. The lady has stealthily held up the bell to silence its telltale jingle so that she is not caught meeting her lover.

Her face is full of conspiratorial anticipation. Above all an outstanding salbhanjika sculpture of pratihara period was recovered from Gyarspur (District Vidisha)[2]. This representative sculpture deserve due appreciation as it exhibits the superb artistic skill achieved by the pratihara artisans of late circa 10th century A.D. The image is shown standing in "Dvibhanga"- posture standing cross legged under the tree, her robe sliding below her naval a distinctive feature of salbhanjika her face an envy and despair for successive generations of connoisseurs who would like to capture her elusive mood.

The image is profusely ornamented with the Puspa Kundala, Ekavali, two series of haras the shorter one is embedded with the diamond beads having three stringed locket suspended with the lotus bud shaped pendants flowing over the abdomen, while the larger hara, with pearl beads, is hanging between her prominent breasts. Her head

---

[1] Plate ...... 50.

[2] Plate ...... 26.

is held at are angle with a slanting regard characterised by laughing charm and an indescribable loveliness.

It is a face and stance that is attractive without being lascivious noble without being supercilious, beautiful with out being fragile. It is one of the unique contributions to the plastic art of India.

The author and painter of Monalisa is known. unfortunately the sculptor of this master piece is not known to us. The lady from Gyraspur has lived for and before the sculptor and she continues to live for us till today.

Mauryan - Sungas - Satvahanas (Buddhist Art)

The Bharhut Stupa of Mauryan period was magnificent structure of art and iconography which gained its popularity all over the Buddhist world. Since it was dilapidated under human bandlism and remains of stupa was buried underneath. In the year 1873 A.D. General Cunningham explored it during his visit. Salvage operations were made and the relics were preserved. The remains of this Stupa was later on displayed in Calcutta Museum Like wise some of the remains were also explored by Shri Jagmohan Vyas the keeper of Allahabad Museum and were displayed by him in the museum.

It is to note that the Stupa of Sanchi is a little later construction than that of Bharhut and Amravati, where in we find there depiction of doctrins of Hinyana pantheon. Symbolic representation of Buddha is the main theme of these stupas, where in four gateways of stupa no. 1 at Sanchi is well carved the expressions of flora, fauna avifauna and acquafauna, in low relief along with various Jotak tales.

In circa 4th century B.C. to Ist century B.C. there was a great development of art and Iconography in vidisha region, where we find large number of yaksa yaksi images were carved in round here, among them anyaksi named shitta was worshiped at chopada is an unique specimen of this period.

The worship of yaksa and yaksis were prevelent in Vidisha, Mathura, Alvi, Patliputra etc.

An image of Yaksi carved out in round in stone from besnagar, have been displayed in Calcutta Museum.

It is more than 6ft high, double plated hair dress, is most representative form of this image.

Like she wears Graveyak, Hara, Katimekhala, nicely tied infront likewise on yaksi image from Kausambi worth mention over here including chamardharni yaksi[1] is representative Icon of the period.

Icons of Sanchi are more important from the point of ancient Indian dress and drapery.

Where in we find that the people of common society were using "Dhoti" Dupatta (Uttarariya) and Indian turban while the ladies were using different kinds of ornaments including a round pendent just above the fore head[2]. The ladies used flowers of various kinds as a local custam tied up in the hairs such Icons have been noticed under Buddhist art.

The faces of the icons of Sunga and Satvahana period are in ovoid shape.

---

[1] Plate - 5 A.

[2] Plate - 5 B.

Kusana Period
(Circa 2nd Century A.D.)

As discussed in the preceding page that the followers of Buddhism worshiped lord Buddha in the form of symbols like "Cakra" "bodhi tree" the Paw of Buddha in abhaya pose etc in the four elaborately carved gateways (torana) was made during the reign of the Satvahanas in the Ist century B.c. as an inscription on the top of architrave of south gateway records the gift of one Anand who was the fareman of the artisans (Avesani) of King Satkarni an early member of the Satvahana dynasty.

Projecting from the abacus of the capitals and supporting the ends of the lowest architraves are the graceful bracket figures of salabhanjikas.

The followers of the Mahayana sect favoured the worship of Buddha in Iconic form.

The artisans of Mathura school of art have represented human and animal fitures.

The forms are elegant and the use of ornament and drapery is kept at a minimum.

The female beauty is the strong point of the Mathura sculptures as illustrated in salbhanjika, garden play (udyan krida) water play (Salil krida).

Mathura artists derived the traditional stock of the tree and animal motifs that were known to their predecessors at Sanchi and Bharhut with their own additions. the forms are elegant and the use of ornaments drapery is kept at a minimum.

The artisan of Mathura were responsible for one of the greatest creation of world's art viz; the Buddha image. For the first time we find here that Buddha is represented in human form[1] the "Iconic form" This image constitutes the most original contribution of Mathura school of art in the field of Indian art. This tradition Continued till 5th century A.D. The image were made in red white spoted sand stones.

Like wise the images of Buddha in human form were sculptured by the artisans in a separate style than that of Mathura. The images of Gandhar art were made from Gandhara stone. The body of the Buddha is covered with the deep wrinkled civara. Buddha images may be divided in to two principal viz; standing[1] (in Samabhanga) and seated (in padmasana). The idea of chakravartin and yogi[2].

Image of Buddha in Gandhar a style is curly hair style half open eyes, sharp nose and multiple folds of drapery in transparent even in stone. facial expression are calm, sharp features with pronounced "Shnisa" and the face is in ovoid shaped consisting a bold Tilak of raised dot.

Buddhist remains noticed in swat valley region of Afghanistion are out standing. There is a Museum in swat where sculptures of Buddha of Gandhar school of art have been preserved.

In this context, it is to point out here that an unique image of Buddha in Gandhar Style rock-cut in bold relief has been preserved in the village "Ghalele" of Swat[3]. A large number of Buddhist stupas were also raised in structural form here. Swat, is well influenced with our

---

[1] Plate -6.

[2] Plate - 7(A).
Plate - 7(B)

[3] Plate - 8.

Sanchi a centre of Buddhism. Swat valley is on way to Khaibarpass in the west. Vajiristhan is located in east-north.

The main aim of the establishment of Gandhara school of art here, was to prepare the Buddha images and for their propagation in for off.

Icons of Gupta age

The Gupta age was marked by an unprecedented intellectual firment and creative upsurage in all branches of art and letters.

It is noteworthy that under the impact of Bhakti cult, which had taken deep root penetrated and permeated all the sects and the society, which necessitated the construction of the shrines. The installation of different deities in the garbhagriha of temples viz;, Siva, Vishnu, Skand and Buddha through out India for worshipers, which were logically provided in Gupta period which s regarded as the pioneer in the field of temple construction.

It is to point out here that sculptural representation is superve. Indeed the sculpture was a thing of joy in life and beyond.

The concept of beauty and grace reached a high watermark during Gupta age. Rasa, Dristi (Emotional concept of eye) became a principal feature of sculpture of this age.

It was the Gupta age when four colosal Buddha images seated in "Padmasana" were enshrined on the four quarters of the great stupa I at Sanchi, in ambulatory passage of it. In this context, it would be useful to refer to what the Bagh caves and their Icons and murals are famous for fine work manship of Gupta age. It can be presumed that feudatories of Gupta Emperors were ruling this region assuming

Imperial titles of "Parambhattaraka" and "Maharajadhiraja" in 4-5th century A.D. under their patromge. Bagh witnessed the art as creativity of "Golden age".

One is convinced that whole region was under the Gupta sovereignty.

Mention may also be made of icons and murals of Ajanta caves are a bit supra sensual rather cold, somewhat austere.

It would be far more correct to hold that a new aesthetic quality, greater verities of postures and mudras defining the divine images Viz; the "Dharma-cakra pravatan mudra" of Buddha, combining knowledge and its analysis both in one posture is a typical example.

Spiritual feeling radiating through the facial expression, explicit elegance calm (Saumya) and balance a greater emphasis on details. Radiating pucker lines of the top postion of the civer (Dholi) a typical characteristic features of Gupta art. Lovely and fine carving details. broad fore head of the images of Gupta period are specific features of Buddha. The eye lids are dropping down like the lotus petals, the eyes are half closed, the eye brows and the eye lids have been shown, demarcated by fine lines in between them. The cheeks are round and bulging out providing long thick lips, long earlobs, fine drapery with curly locks of hair. Such iconographical features resemble with that of icons unearthed in the excavation at Kaushambi (Distt. Allahabad).

These are some of the Iconographical features of Gupta age.

Moreover in late Gupta period i.e. up to 6th century A.D. the sturdiness of the Gupta Icons became more delicate, leading to God looking "Supercilious".

During Gupta period two school of art viz: (i) The Mathura School of art (ii) The Gandhara School of art.

The Iconographical features of the Buddha images of both the schools have been discussed in brief in preceding pages.

The early Buddha images were sculptured in ordinary human form in the prevelent art tradition of Gandhara and Mathura schools.

This art tradition lasted upto 5th cen. A.D./Apart from the Buddhist images as stated above, the unique representative images of Gupta period[1] have been illustrated for our visual reference are:-

- Kumar Kartikeya
  from Gajendra ghat
  District Mandsaur
  4th - 5 th Cen. A.D........ Plate 9

- Kaumari
  from Nanchand
  District Panna
  6th Cen. A.D. .... Plate 10

- Siva Parvati (Displayed
  in Ramvan Museum)
  Satna
  5th-6th Cen. A.D.......... Plate 11

- Maheswari
  from Nanchand
  District, Panna
  6th Cen. A.D............. Plate 12

- Vaishnavi
  from Nanchand
  District Panna
  6th Cen. A.D............ Plate 13

- Indrani
  from Nanchand
  District Panna
  6th Cen. A.D............. Plate 14

Pantheon of Lakulisha

Among the Indian Gods, Siva has attained the prominent place, whose worship was prevelent even in prehistoric period. Such a depiction is found in rock art of various rock shelter of central India.

In Harappa culture Siva was worshiped in "Pasupati" form and linga form.

Rgved refers Siva as "Rudra" Who was not called during performance of a "Yajna" In yajurved, the names of Siva, like Girish kapardi, Shankar, Shambhu, Neellohit etc provide more importance.

According to patanjali, Rudra and Siva forms represent "Pashuna Rudram yajet" and Sivam Rudrasya Bhisji" present a more prominent feature of Siva while Rudra is known as 11th incarntion of Siva.

Apart from the above, Umamaheswara, Mahabhairava form, Bhiksatan form, Ajekpada, Daksina Murti, Yogi form, Siva linga, Lakulisha etc. are prominent forms.

Linga puran vayupuran, refers Lakulisha as the 28th incarnation of Siva.

In the above context, it is to point out here that Kurma and Siva puran provides us information about Lakulisha and various forms of Siva The linga was the primary cult of image, in the early centuries A.D. and the linga dominated images of Siva began to be termed as "Lakulisha".

According to silpatexts the image of Lakulisha must be built in padmasana, holding the danda and vijapuraka, having the erect phallus

"Yogino brahmana vedaparaga urdhvaretas"

Besides these it has also been added that lakulisha should be shown in yoga-Mudra having the yogapatta. Divilingi Lakulisha are also found in various sites of central India. Gajendra ghat (Mandsaur) present a Divilingi Lakulisha belonging to 4th-5th Cen. A.D.[1]

An image of Lakulisha recovered from Satna. belonging, Gupta period 5th cen. A.D. is an unique image[2].

---

1 Plate - 15.

2 Plate - 16.

At Hinglajagarh an image of Lakulisha in Padmasan urdha retas of 8th cen. A.D. is a remarkable image[1] of this period.

Like wise an image of Lakulisha recovered from kharwai (Distt. Raisen) and another image of Lakulisha has been noticed from village Bhagel (Distt Raisen) fixed inside one of nich of a Siva temple.

Apart from the above a large size image of Lakulisha is seen out side the village Sanchet (Distt. Raisen) situated on the bank of a Tank.

Icons of Pratihāra age

The art of the Pratihara age in central India serves as a transition between the post Gupta art and the medieval dynastic art, of major part of Northern and Central India.

In the present context, it is noteworthy that in 8th century pratiharas occupied Central India after the death of Harsa.

Several art centres developed during this period viz Gyaraspur, Badohpathari, Gwalior, Teahi etc. from these centres large number of images of pratihara age have been collected and displayed in Museume of Madhya Pradesh, specially in Gujari Mahal Gwalior, State Museum Bhopal and district Museum Vidisha, among them the representative images like shala bhanjika of Gyaraspur, Uma Maheswara, Ganesh, Vishnu of Vidisha etc. are worth mention over here.

So far as the Iconographical features of the Icons of Pratihara age is concerned, they possess distintive feature and commands a high position.

---

1 Plate - 17.

From the anatomical point of view of the icons of others sects, They possess elongated body. They are adorned with less ornamentations and typical hair style. Ovoid face, long earlobes, thick lips less drapery. In the case of parivar devta for worship and carved round the Garbhagriha of the temple, Sabha mandapa etc, the Sambhanga and in sthanak position, the Gods and Goddesses deities possess minimum quantities of attendants. The female attendant are more sensually depicted in lyrical postures with protruding out breasts.

The image of this age are taller and more rounded and posture is more pronounced, while the nayika images gained more popularity a carved in the facades of Telika Mandir at Gwalior fort, as discussed in preceding pages.

Richly jewelled costumes, head dresses and facial features are distinctly fashioned in Pratihara art. The meticulous depiction of body parts the comparative loss of restraint in exhibtionism, the increase in "Shringar" and other human traits and decline of spiritualism are characteristics in consonance with the emerging feudal ethos of the times.

It is noteworthy that the Icons of Pratihara possess well decorated "Prabhamandala", some of the images with open ornamentation and "ardhaparyankasana" posture, tribhanga posture, varadmudra in sthanak pose like Harihara illustrating fusion of the gods etc are some of the specific featues of the Pratihara Icons.

Iconographical features of the Icons of Pratihara age have been discussed above for our reference. However a few unique reprentative images of pratihara period are illustrated for our adequate under standing.

- Indrani
  From Kota
  District Shivpuri
  7th-8th century A.D........ Plate 18

- Kamadeva
  From Vidisha region
  District Vidisha
  8th Century A.D............. Plate 19

- Natesh Siva (Bhikshatanamurti)
  From Hinglajgrah
  District - Mandsaur
  8th Century A.D. .... Plate 20

- Uma Maheswara
  form Indragarh
  District - Mandsaur
  8th Century A.D........... Plate 21

- Ganesh
  From Keldhar
  District Shivpuri
  8th Century A.D......... Plate 22

- Shalbhanjika
  From Gyaraspur
  District -Vidisha
  9th -10th Century A.D..... Plate 23

- Hari Hara
  From Shivpuri region
  District Shivpuri
  9th-10th Century A.D........ Plate 24

It is notworthy that a number of images of different sect have been found located at various regions of central India Viz; Deogarh, Tumain, Guna, Vidisha, Shivpuri, Sagar, worth mention over here.

One of the unique, representative image of cakresvari has been found displayed in Sahu Sangrahalaya belonging to Pratihara age. As these Icons gained more popularity in the society, a good number of Cakresvari images were carved out by the artisans.

Likewise an images of Vrsabha ruda Uma-Maheswara has been noticed in the village Tumain and another image of Uma Maheswara bearing an inscription of Pratihara age, refering to the name of Vinayak paldeo is found located in the village Rakhetra (Distt. Guna) Simelarly another image of Vishnu in sama padathanak posture has been noticed in the same illage. This unique image is well ornamented.

Likewise an unique image of Natraj has been noticed in the Bhimsen (Distt. Guna) bearing an inscription refering the name of Vinayakpal Deva a Paratihara King.

Some interesting seated image of Vishnu has been found on the lalatbimba of the temple at Badoh- Pathari (Distt. Vidisha) and Bhainswaha (Distt. Sagar) espectiely. Both the temples belong to the pratihara age.

Another beautiful image of (Vishnu) Vaman Avtar Image has been found, asignable to circa 8th cen. A.D of pratihara age from Badoh Pathari (Vidisha), Displayed in Central Archaeological Museum Gwalior.

In district Museum Vidisha is seen displayed a similar image of Vaman, worth mention over here.

Icons of Parmāra age

The origin of Parmara dynasty is controversial, however it was a powerful Rajput family of 10th century A.D. The first king of this family was Upendra who was the founder of the Parmara dynasty. In fact he was chief of the Rashrakutas and Gurjara Partiharas[1].

In due course of time, this dynasty fell into the struggle with Rashrakutas. The suceeeding rulers like Vakpati Raj, Munj, Sindhuraj, Bhoja, Udyaditya and Narvarman provided Stability to the kingdom.

The Parmara empire reached to its zenith under. Soveregnty of Bhoja with his capital at Dhara. He was a great builder and patron of arts and staunch worshiper of Saraswati the famous sculpture of Bhojsala Saraswati temple at Dhar beloning to this age is displayed in British Museum London.

---

[1] Sharma R.K. - Madhya Pradesh-ke-Puratativa ka Sandarbha Granth Bhopal 1974- P- 70

This period was of great temple construction acticity. These temples were now not only places of worship but also centres of Social and cultural life too.

In this context it is to point out here that parmaras constructed number of gigantic temple with exquisit sculptures carved in relief's at Omkar Mandhata (Distt. Khandwa) Un (Distt. Khargone), Hinglajgarh (Distt. Mandsaur) Nemawa (Disst. Dewas), Udaipur (Distt. Vidisha) Gandharvapuri (Distt Dewas), Ashapuri (Distt. Raisen) and Ujjain.

The outstanding Icons of Gauri, Uma-Maheswara Narsingha etc. have been displayed in the Museums of Madhya Pradesh Viz: Bhanpura Museum, Mandsaur, Indore, Bhopal, Ashapuri (Open Air Museum) Gandharvapuri (Open Air Museum and Birla Museum at Bhopal).

In this reference, it is to point out that some of the stray Icons now displayed in the museum, need appreciation.

A colossus image of Brahmanical Trinity of Vishnu which was collected from the ruins of the temples of Ashadevi at Ashapuri is worth mention over here, it is now preserved in vaishnava gallery of Birla Museum Bhopal.

So far as the Icons of 8th and 9th century A.D. and Subsiquent age and sculptures of medieval Malwa from 10th Century onwords it may be studies in reference to Omkar Mandhata (Amareswara temple) Bhojpur, Sandhara, Kethuli, Jharda, Makla (10 Cen. A.D.) Un, Uddaypur (1059-1080 A.D.), Jamli (Dhar district) 11th Cen. A.D. Nemavar and Ramgarh (12th Cen. A.D.).

Though structured within the earlier classical idioms the Parmara art shows regional specification of its own. The ethos of the times, tendencies of ostentatious display and frotic etc. get reflected in a great emphasis on ornamentation, foliation, and scroll work. The Icons are elaborate and beautifully integrated through the naturalism of the

Gupta age has given way to more for malistic style and code Finer details of ornamentation under the parmaras reached a high degree of sophistication with varieties of necklaces.

The betel leaf shaped beads and other jewels that have been used in necklaces and other ornaments is the specific feature of the Icons.

Like wise the necklace passing round the breasts of male and protruding breasts of the female divinities is one of the district feature of the Icons of Parmara age.

A Considerable number of Icons of Parmara age and remains of shrines and sculptures in situ assigned to the early medieval period of Indian History prove the prevalence of Iconic worship in Madhya Pradesh.

It is interesting to mention over here that at village Sonari near Udaipur (District Vidisha) a large number of Parmara images have been discovered from a field near keotin river in June 2009 in which the outstanding image of vishnu pl.28 and master piece gigantic imge of yajna varah (Iconic form) are the unique finding of this region.

Iconographical features of Icons of parmara age have been discussed above the district representative master piece images of parmara age are illustrated for our adequate under standing:

- Ravananugrha Murti
  from Hinglajgarh (Mandsaur)
  11th Century A.D........ Plate 25

- Abhisarika
  From Hinglajgarh (Mandsaur)
  11th Century A.D........... Plate 26

- Gauri
  From Hinglajgarh (Mandsaur)
  11th Century A.D........ Plate 27

- Vishnu
  Newly discovered
  from Sunari village (Vidisha)
  11th Century A.D......... Plate 28

- Uma Maheswara
  from Hinglajgarh (Mandsaur)
  11th Century A.D...... Plate 29

- Shakti Ganesh
  Mandsaur
  11th Century A.D.......... Plate 30

- Parvati
  Bhanpura (Mandsaur)
  11th Century A.D....... Plate 31

- Hari Hara (Seated in ardhaparyankasaxa)
  from Hinglajgarh (Mandsaur)
  11th Century A.D............ Plate 32

- Uma Maheswara
  from Hinglajgarh (Mandsaur)
  11th Century A.D........ Plate 33

- Uma- Maheswara
  from Barud (Bhind)
  11th Century A.D............ Plate 34

- Kartikeya (Sthanaka Image)
  from Hinglajgarh (Mandsaur)
  11th Century A.D............ Plate 35

- Hari-Hara (Sthanaka)
  from Hinglajgarh (Mandsaur)
  11th Century A.D............. Plate 36

- Vishnu
  from Vidisha
  12th Century A.D.............. Plate 37

- Jain Chatustika
  from Phupher (Vidisha)
  12th Century A.D.......... Plate 38

Icons of Kalcuri age

The Kalcuris of Dahalamandal whose capital was Tripuri (Tewar), district Jabalpur were also the chiefs in the beginning but rose into power during circa 8th century A.D. They are supposed to have migrated from Mahishmati (Modern Mandhata of district Khargone)[1].

---

[1] Sankalia. H.D. - In search of three cities Journal Madhya Pradesh Parised, Vol III, P. 178, Bhopal, 1955.

After they settled it Tripuri, the family was divided in to three branches viz; the Kalcuris of Tripuri, the Kalcuris of Ratanpur and Kalcuris of Sarayupar, known as cedimandala or dahalamandala Tripuri house was more powerful and ruled over an extensive empire from Circa 8th century A.D. to 13th century A.D.

Vamaraja the founder of Kalcuri dynasty of Tripuri was also known as successor of Budharja of Mahishmati, Sankaragana I, the ruler of Tripuri acquired an imperial title. other rulers of this dynasty were Lakshmanraja, Kokal I, Sankargana II, Yuvraja Deva I, Lakshaman Raja II, Sankaragana III Yuvrajadeva II, Kokala II, Gangegadeva and Karan, Who ruled from 9th century A.D. to 11th century A.D. Among them Gangeyadeva and Karan were great warriors. They extended their empire after capturing the other territories. They were great builders and constructed several temples with sculptures and developed many centres like, Gurgi, Bilahari, Bhelaghat, Chandreh, etc.

Rulers of Kalcuri dynasty were saivites, they took interest in other sects also.

The circular temple of Bhedaghat known as Golkimath also called Chausath Yagini temple, a centre of Tantric cult is a noteworthy feature of this region. The queen of Yuvrajadeva I Known as Nohla, Contributed a lot in building the temples etc. Yuvrajadeva I is credited to have developed a centre at Gurgi near Rewa, and Constructed a large temple and Matha, where Matamayur branch of Saiva gained more popularity.

Kalcuri art is distinguished by an unprecedented eye for detail so, much so that the relief often looks crowded and unwieldy.

It is noteworthy that Kalcuries were immediate successors of vakatakas in Deccan and hence their art forms are influenced by the vakataka tradition. Religious syncretism was the dominant features of society during Kalcuris and influenced both the subject and style of depiction.

The Kalcuri Icons denote a new facial type, squaresh with projected chins, Swollen Cheeks and closed eyes.

The short features and structured proportion of the body, sharp turns (Bitriangular) on axis of the body structure are some other featres of Kalcuri art forms.

The human figures show a delicate elongated body type with a hand some oval face, which characterize developed Kalcuri sculpture.

The personal and social ideas and customs prevelent in society during the times get successful representation in kalcuri Icons.

In case of Tridev Icons of Kalcuri age, the Prabhamandala of Vishnu, there is no decoration while in the case of Brahama and Siva it is adorned with flowers. The depiction of Trideva in Icons of Kalcuri is rare. the Characteristic features of Kulcuri style are vivid in facial construction and other motifs.

The sculptures depicted in the temples are :-

Human figures including figures of attendents, devotees etc.

Animal figures architectural designss mythical figures like makara.

Apart from the other decorations of carvings are :-

Architectural decorations.

Geometrical pattern designs

Floral designs

So far as we have discussed above about the iconographical features of Icons of Kalcuri age, however the representative Icons of

Kalcuri age depicting the iconographical features are illustrated here as the unique theme and the detailed treatment of the Icons make it a masterpiece.

- Trideva
  from Mankhedi (Jabalpur)
  10th Century A.D.......... Plate 39

- Uma-Maheswara
  from Jabalpur
  10th Century A.D........ Plate 40

- Vaisnavi
  from Dhubela
  11th century A.D...... Plate 41

- Vaman
  from Semaria (Shahdol)
  11th Century A.D....... Plate 42

- Krisna Janma
  from Shahdol
  11th Century A.D...... Plate 43

- Yogini
  from Shahdol
  12th Century A.D........ Plate 44

- Skhalit Vasna
  from Jabalpur
  13th Century A.D........ Plate 45

Icons of Candellas age

The Candellas, whose origin in controversial, were the chiefs ruling under the imperial Gurjara Pratiharas in 9th cen. A.D. and availed the opportunity of weak sovereign. Obviously they attempted to establish their supremacy over their overlord and also the contemporary Rajput ruler of Northern India.

Harsa the candella king consoli dated his position and assumed an imperial title.

Yasovarman the son and successor of Harsa was the next ruler of this family whose flowing account of achievements are given in Khajuraho stone inscription of his son Dhang[1].

Yasovarman was a great warrior who defeated various rulers and extended the boundaries of has empire.

The prominent rulers of this dynasty are Dhangadeva, Ganda, Vidyadhara, Kirtivarman and parmardideva. They were great builders and connoisseurs of art and architecture.

The power of the candellas reached its zenith under the most ambitious ruler Dhanga (950-1008 A.D.) The temples of Khajuraho, which due to their sculptural ornamentation, are regarded as the best and most celebrated examples of early medieval art. Brilliant in conception and grace, the many tiered sculptures are not only "exquisite" in workmanship, but vitality, ornamentation and details make one dumb struck.

In keeping with the early medieval feudalistic society and norms, the Iconic art of candellas underlines the triumph of the sensuous over sublime.

---

[1] E.I. Vol (I. P- 121-125).

The spiritualism of Gupta period has now been transformed into a celebration of the physical side of love. Shringar, mithuna and rati are the central themes of many such sculptures and varieties of this theme are carved out in details. Various Icons carved in relief may, however be divided into five groups.

The first group of sculptures are of Gods and Goddesses. These were meant for worship in the temples carved in bold relief. Generally these images are in "Samabhanga" and some of them are giagantic and they are installed inside temples.

The second group of images belong to "Parsva Devata" or Parivara images. There have been carved or fixed over the facade or in niches. viz Dikpalas, Ganas and Jain Shasan devtas etc.

The third group of Icons are of Sur-Sundaris or "Apsaras". These images are large in number and have been depicted in attractive poses in standing ati bhanga posture, playing with a ball (Kanduka Krida). The Twisted body is one of the typical posture of Srinagara which was in vouge during this period at Khajuraho. The apsaras are adorned with Kundala, Kangana, Katimekhala, nupura etc as ornaments and a transparent sari thus augmenting the erotic mood. Such erotic (Mithun) images at Khajuraho indicate the influencing Kaulkapalik sects. There are Naikas in an amazing poses. Some tie bells on their ankles for a dance or play on flutes and trumpets, some stretch their limbs in infinite languor, while others squcez their hair dry after bath. Their robs sliding down to reveal their exquisite charm (Skhalit Vasna Nayika) one squeeses her legs right in unbearable passion, while another pouts before a mirror. The ranging passion of erotic Nayika has found rest in material compassion and fulfilment of the Vatsala Nayika holding her child.

The fourth group of images that have been carved, relates to social life of present day.

The fifth group present the images of animals and birds. Among the animals, the "Shardula" a horned lion is prominent representation.

The phisiography of Icons at Khajuraho displays certain characteristic features, like carved eyes, eyebrows, nose and lips.

Depiction of "Saumya", Ugra, Samhara, Sukhasana, and Nrtya Murtis of Siva along with other Gods, Goddesses and secular images dealing with various walk of life and occupations have turned Khajuraho into an open Air museum of art gallery of India.

Interestingly is the fact that Khajuraho was one of main kapalik centre where ratichakra mahotsava was the main function of the Kapalikas. Such erotic images depiction is an attraction of General man, as discussed above, those images reflect the hold of Kaul and Kapalika sects here.

Representation of tantric rituals like in temples of Orissa (Sun temple Konark) Puri, Bhuvneshwara and Bhoramdeo temple (District Kawardha) are the flourishing trends of the Kaul Kapalik sects in those days.

A few representative Icons of Candella period depicting the iconographic features are illustrated here by-

- Siva (Sambhanga)
  Darpan Naiyka and erotic image
  from Khajurah
  10-11th Century A.D........ Plate 46

- Apsara
  From Khajuraho
  11-12th century A.D....... Plate 47

- Apsara
  from Khajuraho
  11-12th Century A.D......... Plate 48

- Avlokiteswara
  from Mausania
  (Chhatarpur)
  10th Century A.D........... Plate 49

Icons of Kachhapaghāta age

The Kachchapaghata dynasty was established in northern part of central India in the vicinity of Gwalior by king Vajradaman, who was the first king of Kachchapaghata family and he captured Gopadri fort (Gwalior fort) in 10th Century A.D.

In fact that Kachchapaghata rulers were great builders. The great Siva temple at sohania was built by this dynasty, like wise the constuction of large Siva temple at padhavali goes to their credit.

In Mitavali the circular temple in plan is one of the representative temples of India.

In the year 1085-1093 padmapala and Ratnapala ruler of Kachahapaghata built a large Padmanath temple at Gwalior fort called Bada Sas-Bahu temple and small Sas-Bahu temple respectively. Suhania was the great centre of Kachchapaghata art. Other prominent rulers of this dynasty were Muladeva, Devpala, Padmpala and Mahipala. Two other branches of Kachchapaghata dynasty ruled from Narwar and Dubkunda.

The prominent features of Kachchapaghata Icons are, the sharp facial profiles with elongated noses and full, sensuous looking lips.

These seems to be an amalgamation of the classical percepts with the socio cultural milieu of the early medieval times where worldly concerns and persuits shaped both the patrons and the craft.

The influence of Tantric cult beliefs is also Visible here. Even the Jain images in the Kachchapaghata period look less ascetic. Passion and intensity of life are vividly portrayed in kachchapaphata art though a variety of bhangas and bhangimas which provide a dynamism to the Icons.

Apart from the iconographical features of Kachchapaghatas, the uniqe masterpices have been illustrated for our visual reference are :-

- Siva
  from Barhad (Bhind)
  11th Century A.D........... Plate 50

- Adinath
  from Narwar (Shivpuri)
  12th Century A.D........... Plate 51

- Vaishnavi
  from Shivpuri
  11-12th Century A.D........... Plate 52

- Ambika
  from Shivpuri
  11-12th Century A.D........... Plate 53

- Vishnu Vishvarupa
  Suhania (Morena)
  10th Century A.D........... Plate 54

- Alas Nayika
  from Morena
  10th Century A.D........... Plate 55

- Buddha
  (Bhumisparsa Mudra)
  from Keldhar (Shivpuri)
  10th Century A.D........... Plate 56

On our close study of the Icons of different sects illustrated above, we can easily pointout that silpis carved very carefully the faces of icons which are normally circular/oval shaped. The protected chin, as well as the sharpness in the execution the eye-brows, eye lids the lips and nose respectively.

Likewise the heavy breasts (Protruding out) and thigh portion for giving the final touch. We may however presume that the silpis of ancient India were particular who fashioned these Icons in a high skill and perfect manner.

3

ICON WORSHIP, TANTRICCULT AND TANTRIC CENTRES OF ANCIENT INDIA

The most noteworthy features of iconographic representation of worship is Icon. The Icons are made with the basic aim of being worshiped discussed in chapter-2 Image worship is an out come of devotional sentiments from oneself. The devotee (Bhakta), during his course of devotion, completely surrenders before the lord (his ist deva) and prays or begs in so manyways, reciting hymns (Prathana slokas or Mangala sloka etc.for the welfare of one and every one.

Basic concept of auspiciousness is as old as the development of man hiself.

It is to mention over here that the vedic literatre being the earliest record as literature in India which enumerate all our customs, beliefs religious, practices and so many rituals and traditions etc. In an orthodox belief all the Vedic hymas are considered to be a sort of prayer and therefore quite auspicious in their nature. The basic features, elements or germs of the later age benedictory verses are also available there. It is possible, that on this very lineage developed the custom of begining any work with prayer to the gods or goddesses of ones on faith. As a matter of fact the production of hymns of praise to the gods naturally didnot cease with Vedic poets[1] but was more keenly followed by the authors or poets of the later periods.

Unlike other world religions such as christianity, Islam, Buddhism, Hindusm didnot have any one founder . It grew gradaally over a period of five thousand years absorbing and assimilating all the religious and culttural movements of India. The Vedas, the Upanishads, the Gita, the Ramayana, the Mahabharat, the Puranas the books on the So-called "Six Systems of Philosphy the songs of the Bhakti movement and the mystics are all authoritative, but non is exclusively so saiva thought and philosphy by itself a complete system of thought of Siva is an important God whose antiquity linked with mythology, created bewilderingly rich and varied philosophical musings. He is the creator preserver, a well as destroyer or absorber. He is the lord of all being Pasunam patih, a great lord (Mahadeva) Maheswara, the supreme God. The element of superiority or Siva as a lord par excellence has survived through centuries down to this day.

The worship of Siva goes as far back as 3000 B.C. Signs of the cult of the mother Goddess and the phallic cult have been found in these civilization.

Linga worship has been of wide prevalence in the ancient world. We meet with the vestiges of it in India. Ancient Egypt, Syria, Babylon, among the Assyrians in Persia, Greece and ther, European conutries and in different parts of America, Mexico, Peru and Haiti on account of its close association with Siva the phallic cult has assumed a significant role in the religious history of India.

---

[1] Keith, History of Sanskrit literature PP 210.

Siva is worshipped in the symbol of "Linga" and also in the anthropomorphic form. Various types of Siva lingas and their clasification is known to us from various Siva Agams and other texts. In mansara Suprabhedagmas and Kamikagama different kinds of "Linga" have been classified. According to the Kamikagama the Sthavar (immovable) lingas are grouped in to six heads the svambhuva the Daivika, the Arshaka, the Ganpatya, the Manusha and the Bana-Linga of these, the Svaymbhyva are said to belong the uttamottama (Most superior) Variety of Lingas. The text describes the Svambhuva linga as one which rose up and came into existence by itslf and had existed from time immemorial. Sixtyeight places which are situated in various parts of India are said to possess Svambhuva lingas and list of Places is given in the Commentary on his Jirnodhara Dasakam by Nigamajnandeva of Vyaghrapura, son of Vamadevsivacharya.

Under different trends of art and Iconography, symbolic worship was in vogue during Hinyana phase of worship.

Later on during Mahayan Buddhist faith worshipers of Buddha hed greatdesire for Iconic form and there was high pressure among the common mass and when the devotees of Buddha came into power with the result the images of Buddha were fashined under Mathura school of art and Gandhar school of art for worshiping of Buddha in anthropomorphic form.

It may be mentioned again that in Indian art Siva appeared first on coins and seals in the form of Linga and not in human form. The Linga of Siva was regarded as his symbol. This symbol reflects the most powerful form of Siva and Ominipotent. He was considered bene volent creater of universe and destruction.[1]

---

[1] Lingapurana P- 73, 2-6.

The earlier anthropomophic representation of Siva akin to the Greek god is a striking feature common. As discussed above that as Mahayana was a very popular religion and led to the origin and development Buddha image in human form therefore the Brahmanists conceived the idea of creating the material form of Siva in human form basing their concepts on illusions of the Vedas.

The period of circa 3rd- 2nd century B.C. may be regarded the genesis and development and anthropomorphic representation of Hindu Gods and Goddesses.

From the close study of the ancient Icons, it appears that the worshipping of gods in human form become prevelent from few centuries of Christian era.

The most important and earliest anthropomorphic representation of Siva is seen at Gudimallam in circa 3rd century B.C. Where a large Siva- linga, Whose front part bears Siva standing in human form, with two arms having battle-axe, cut into bold relief, standing on the sholders of the curshing figure which may be identified with aparmarapurusa.

This Siva linga appears like a phallus which in a way confirms the theory that Siva linga represents the organ of Siva.

This Linga has clear influence of the Tantric religion. Though the period of development of Tantric cult was much later. From this itappears that Tantric philosophy existed in India much earlier. It is well known fact that there was a great influence of Tantric cult in south India than in the North.

On some early representations of Siva has been depicted with horns. In Archacological Museum Lucknow a Siva-linga of red sand stone bears the anthropomorphic representation of Siva in northern style. This image is ascribed Kusana period.

The Karamadanda stone linga of the region of Gupta emperor Kumar Gupta-I, belonging to 5th century A.D. represent a Manusa Linga.

According to Siva Purana, the Manusa-Linga depict three parts viz; Brahma bhaga (Square), Visnu Bhaga (Octagonal) and Rudrabhaga (Cylindrical)

In the early phase of development of anthropomorphic froms of Icons, they were sculptured human form mostly with two hands in the begining, later on the hands and attributes began multi plying.

The Aihole sculptures of Vrsavahana murti of Siva represents him with four arms standing in dvibhanga- mudra, resting on his vrsabha holding Trisula, snake and one hand in Varadamudra, granting boon of life of deities.

One of the asana type image is also found having four arms, three faces seated in Sukhasuna on his Nandi. This is the earliest asana type of image of Siva.

It will not be out of place to mention that the phallic form of Siva has thus been the commonest form of worship adopted by saivites in ancient India.

Apart from the linga worship and Mukhalingas the other Icons like Rudra, Lakulisa, Natraja, Anugra Murtis Kalyan Sunder, Ardhanariswara, Dandadhara Siva, Uma-Maheswara, Sada Siva, Trimurti, Bhairava and Ganesh Icons etc. have been worshiped.

A few representative image of different sects for worship have been illustrated here. Sakti-cult viz, saptamatrikan, Parvati, Durga, Mahisasur- Mardini, Brahmani, Vaisnavi Varahi, Indrani, Kaumari, Maheswari and Chamunda etc are a few to quote here with. So far as the anthropomorphic form of Siva is concerned sometimes the image of Siva is found sitting in a mood of relaxation with parvati and flanked by his sons Kumar Kartikeya and Ganesh and the dwarf like ganas while the (personified) Ganga, the sun and moon are quietly looking at them together with the attendant guards and maid. A large number of panels representing the manifold aspects of the divinity and claiming reverence for the deity who is more widely worshiped than Visnu in southern India.

Like Panchmukhi Mahadeva in which four headed Siva linga with central part being Iswara is a theme of great worship such an image pasupathinath is worshiped in Kathamandu Nepal and another image of identical features belonging to Gupta period is worshiped in Mandsaur.

The four central deities of Hindu Pantheon later on resorved into, Trimurti form of deity for worship, namely Visnu, Brahma, Surya and Siva[1].

Besides a few examples of composite form of deities, the Hindu god heads and multiple forms, the various Gods and godesses were not regarded as separate and competing entities.

They are different aspects of same central deity seen in one or other of His innumerable forms and qualities[2].

For our visual inter cession, Siva in Natraja form symbolises his five fold function or the panch-kriyas, viz; creation, Preservation, Destruction, Removal of Ignorance and Ensuring communion with the Divine, in an eternal chain of time in course of his ceaseless gyration through the medium of "Cosmic Dance"

---

[1] Havell.E.B., The art heritage of India P. 151 Footnote I.

[2] Iyer K. Brahma, Indian art P.2.

The composite form of deities whatever we may give the name whether male or female, the oneness of all of them for worship viz; Ardhanariswara, a combined form of Siva and Parvati, like wise Trinity of Hari- Harakka image (Vishnu, Siva and Surya) and Hari-Hara (Visnu-Siva) Trideva (Brahma, Visnu and Siva) etc.

Surya is one of the important vyantara devatas of Hinduism. It is the visible celestial luminary was being worshipped in India from the earliest times. The evidence of Sun Worship in the Indus valley civilization has been accepted.

The vedas (Rgvida and other contemporary texts) refer to him and his various aspects as Savir, Pusan, Bhaga, Vivasvat, Mitra, Aryaman and Visnu. Surya was the most concrete of the solar deities and Savitr "the stimulator of every thing" (Sarvasya Prasavita- Nirukta).

Surya has also been mentioned as "dvadasdita" in puranas and Brahmana lexts. In the begining sun might have been represented in Indian art by means of different symbols like the Swarnapatra, Ka-malapuspa, Chakra, Vartula etc. Most probably the magas who migrated from Iran to India introduced The sun worship in India in Iconographic forms. We find specific details of surya images in the "Brahatsamhita".

In this context it would be useful to refer to the Trividha Sakti creator - These three powers of the sun are Pranda, Arogyda, and Divyada, balancing the nature.

Several extant art motifs of the Gandhara region, and Mathura, belonging to the early centuries of the Christian era, help us to trace the development of the new and re-orientated surya icons of the Gupta and post Gupta periods.

A small figure of Surya in black stone found in one of the sites of Gandhara shows the god seated at easy on a chariost drawn by fours horses. The Sun god bears gum boot and attended by a female figure on either side.

In the tantric texts surya and his attributer are Interpreted in the following way.

Surya in the very self of Atman traveling in chariot of living beings. The wheel is the very self of time the seven horses are the life- impluses of creatures the consciousness, energy karman, activity, intellect strength, discrimination. The all prevader, seated on a luminous seat, travels across the whole world constituted by the three gunas. The Karmans, Composed of Sattva, Rajas and tamas he holds tight with his reins.

The reins are mind (means) the driver of the chariot is illumination or discrimination (Prajna) Arun, who has a head, and upper part, but is befret of feet. The adept yogin worships bhaskara as the celestial void (Nabhah Sunya). The great void (Maha Sunya) the self luminous void (Taijasa Sunya).

In preceeding pages we have given a glimpse of worship of Icons of Saiva cult as well as those of Hinyana and Mahayana phase of worship of Icons of Buddha.

Vaisnava cult under the Brahmanical religion possessed a commanding position. The worship of Visnu got a high position. In Rgveda has been mentioning the Visnu as "Aditya[1]", being treated an ordinary got at the time of begining of vaisnav cult. Gradually, during the later vedic period the importance of Visnu as per the details enlightened in the satapatha. Brahmana and the Taittriya Aranyaka[2].

---

[1] Rgveda 1, 155, 5, 7, 99.2.

[2] Suryakant, Vedic Devasastra (The Hindi Translation of the Vedic Mythology by Macdonell), Delhi 1961, P. 94.

Later on, in epics and puranic age Visnu got the highest position among the Brahmanical triad, Viz; Brahma, Visnu and Mahes'a i.e. " Trideva", the gods of creation, preservation and destruction respectively and composite form of Visnu is an outcome of the coordination of all the three divinities.[1]

It is to mention over here that after Siva worship (Phallus and Icon), the other most powerful hindu god is Visnu, who has formed the subject of many benedictory verses from inscriptions.

Visnu got the name upendra (i.e. next of Indra) during early Vedic period.

After a long span of time of religious history became Such a popular god that by the Gupta period, Visnu had easily superceded Indra and other hindu divinities and acquired the name of Atindra.[2]

It is to not that Visnu and his cult were made from as early as the 2nd century B.C. Garudadhaj pillar of Besnagar (Vidisha) is a Testimony of supreme popularity of Vaisnav cult during this age. Heliodoraous pillar inscription[3]. Provides such information.

In the Iconographic domain, Visnu, like Siva, has not only some peculiar forms to be depicted but also his more than ten incarnations, takeup a good deal more space than that of Siva.

Most probably, the depiction of Visnu in Icon form began during Kusana period, In Mathura Museum some of the Icons of Visnu are preserved.

Thus a few representative image of Visnu cult viz Sthanaka image of Maha Visnu in Katyavalambita pose, image of Visnu in

---

[1] Awasthi R. - Khujuraho Ki Deva Pratimaya, Agra, 1961. P.50

[2] Visnu - Sahastranama, Verse - 30, Gorakhpur edition.

[3] Hiliodorus pillar inscription- Siear D.E. Select inscriptions P. 88

Sampadasthanka pose Among Asana murtis of Visnu in yogasana, Lalitasana, and Garudasana, Laksmi, and Laksmi-Narayana Sayan Murtis of Visnu like Sesasayina-Visnu,

It is significant to mention that only a few of the Dasavatara image, like, Vraha, Nrsimha, Sankarsana Balram, Krisna and Matsya and Vaman Avtara have been displayed in Dasarna- region.

Apart from the above syncretistic Icons of Visnu like Hari-Hara, Trideva etc. have also been found for worship.

Some important Icons of various sects have also been illustrated here meant for worship.

Tantric Cult and Tanric Centres of Ancient India

In the field of Iconography as well as religious literature, indicates the terrible form of Siva was uitilized by Tantrist. Looking to this where many times the terms like Kapali, Kapardin, Goramukha, Bhairava, Sarva, Sadasiva and Virupaksa were used in some places for the same deity.

Faint traces of Tantrism, however, can be found in the text and inscriptions of the Gupta period. The very word Tantra occurs in an inscription found in a village Gangdhar (Jhalabad) where in is depicted about the abode of (divine mothers), filled full of Dakinis who stir up very occans with the mighty wind rising from the Tantric rites of their religion.[1]

[1] C.I.I., Vol III P-78.

The person who well versed in Madala Krama, entitled to install the images of divine mothers, might have been Tantric Sakti worshippers.

In the medeaeval period Tantrism associated with Brahmanical Hinduism as well as mahayanas or vajrayan form of Buddhism attained full development in India. The Tantric cult being specially predominent in eastern India. Sakti worship was also popular among many Hindus of extreme south west of India. Sankarcharya the great exponent of Advaitavada, was a great worshipper of the Goddess. He is said to have composed in her honour the famous. Tantric text "Saundaryalahari".

After the decline of Buddhist faith from Indian Soil and also the incredible growth of Tantrism in it, this growth happened also in the case of saiva faith under the galaxy of eminent teachers of mattamayura cult, the most dominent cult of pasupatas during circa 10th-11th century A.D. in northern India. The more staunch followers of Tantrism in Buddhist faith may have been partially absorbed by the not very dissimilar pasupatas, where as the softer section may have switched over to join faith, which, with its severity had kept up the purity of faith in a good meusure from the degenerating influence of Tantrism. The main stay of the saner "middle path" of the Buddha Viz the Sreshthis (rich traders) and Grihapati. could not swallow the contradiction presented by the Tantric rituals of later Mahayana Buddhism and this spelled the doom of that cult.

It will not be out of place here to pat a few words about the worship of Saktis which was incorporated by the popularisation of Tantric religion of Malwa and that is why the Sakti worship was accompanied by Tantric practices under the parmaras[1]. Thus the Tantrism hold the belief of a considerable portion of population.

[1] Bajpai K.D. And Rao M. Catalogue of Devi gallery, Birla Museum Bhopal P.1.

Like wise during candella dynastey Buddhism and Tantrism was pevelent and many of the magnificent Jaina and Buddhist temple are still wetnessing the Icons of Buddha and Buddhist goddess Tara[1], with existence of Tantric cult.

Interestingly is the fact that Khajuraho was one of main Kapalik centre where ratichakara mahotraa was the main function of Kapalikas, where in the erotic images reflect the hold of Kaul and Kapalika sects here.

Representation of Tantric rituals like in temples of Orissa (Sun Temple Konark) puri Bhavneswara are the flourishing trends of Kaul Kapalik sects in those days. The yogini-pithas were established when the Brahmanical tantric religion became very popular in the society and gained popularity with the Vajrayana sect of the Buddhists of 6-7th century A.D. odrapitha, being the first Tantric pitha in India according to the Kalikapuran which was flourished in the coastal region of Orissa near Puri and in Madhya Pradesh having its centres first at Ranipur, Jhariyal, then at Bheraghat, where in we find monuments of different ages.[2]

The Kaul sect was propagated by Matsyendra nath, it was an another form of Sakta sect.

In this context it will be useful to know that in the medieval period the sakta sect was transformed in to Kaul sect.

A body of the Tantric texts and similar number of shrines found in various part the country clearly indicate and reveal that several inexhaustible attempts made by its exponents and followers went a long

---

[1] M.A.S.I. No. 8

[2] Mohapatra K. A note on the Hypaethral temple of sexty four yogini at Hirapur, Orissa. The Orissa Historical Research Journal Vol II, 1953, P-36-41

way to popularize this esoteric cult between the 9th and 12th century A.D. and the erotic Icons got more significance between along span period 7th century A.D. to 13th century A.D. it is because of silpis got influence of Kamsutra of Vatrayan and these silpis fashioned number of erotic images on the facade of the temples In circa 7th century A.D. the "Dyvatbad" (Purus) and "Adyvatebad" (Prakriti) merged in one, as seen the various temples and the tradition of sculpering the "Mithana (Erotic) image by silpis as a tradition.

In the first phase of medieval period, the two sects viz; Saiva sect and Sakta sects remained in struggle for Nibratta (Yoga) and Abratta (Bhoga), this resulted the meeting ground of both sects in the various temples only because it was difficult to differentiate their views.

Kaula sect was worshiper of Sakti, while the Saktas got great faith on Siva and Saktiboth.

The well known "Panchamkar" of Kulas gained more popularity, in which the following things were used viz; Mudra (roasted grain) "Matsya" (fish), mas (meat), Madira (wine), and sexual (inter course (maithuna). A good number of historical texts mention that to attain "Siddhi" (spiritual power), the sadhakas (the Tantric worshipers) unanimously offered flesh, blood and wine to the yoginis a tradition is still in practice in several parts of Orissa. Devotees offer all these things to most of the village goddesses on important festive occasions, in the times of crises and each time these goddesses manifest themselves in dream or otherwise to the devotees, demanding such scarifies.

Mention may be made of the cakra, alternatively known as "Yogini cakra", Kaula cakra (the circle of time) or the Bahiravi cakra (the circle of Bhairavi) the woman companion of the terrifying from of Siva knowns s "Bhairava" The "Marga" or path that defines five ways to perform penance to attain liberation and happiness, discussed above.

During the worship the worshippers used to carry the female with them. According to Kudarnava Tantra" (8,5/5) the woman is denoted Cakra wine and meat are the worship and sexual intercource of man is prosides path of moksa. Thus in the name of Siva and Sakle "kamakala" and ritual worship came into existence.

The sect of Kaplikas in identical with of Kaulas. This sect was propagated by "Siddha Kandapa" At the time of worship the woman which was taking part, was called "Kapal Vanita"

The famous text of "Bhavbhuti maltimadhava, refers to a famous Kapalika Aghorghant and his Kapal vanita kapal kundala, respectively. The worship of these is called Rati cakra Mohostava where Rati (female) and cakra (yoni, the female genitalia) are the components of worship. At the time of worship of image of Sakti or Tara, the Kapalika used to take the skull full of wine in one hand and dance in circle alongwith his Kapalvanita and the "sexual intercourse" was also taken place.

The Rati cakra Mahotsava" an important ritual was the main aim of worship of Kapalika to obtain "Moksa".

Central India was an important region where Tantric practices were prevelent since ancient times specially in "Daksina-Kosala" region presently covering districts of Raipur, Durga, Bastar, Bilaspur, Rajnadgaon, Surguja, and Raigarh of present chhattisgarh and a part of sambalpur of Orissa.

A reference to the origin of Sakta cult in Ancient India is made in Virata paran of Mahabhrata where goddess Durga is said to have her perpetual abodein Vindhya mountain.

Daksina-Kousal is closely located to Vindhya region. The spread of the Sakti cult from the place of origin to its adjoining area may easily be surmised.

According to Siva Mahapuran[1] the important Sakti-worship centre was at Amarkantaka, Ujjain the "Gathasaptasati" also refers to a female kapalin. The above references substantiate that this period the Kaul-Kapalika sects of saivism existed in Daksina-Kosala also.

The important Tantic centres of Ancient India

So far we have discussed about the location of Tantric centres in "Daksina Kosala" region in preceding page. However the following Tantric centres have been found located in various states of India.

The Kamakhya

The Kamakhya temple is one of the famous Sakta temple of India and is regarded as one of the main centres of Tantrism.

Kamakhya is at the centre of the widely practiced, powerful tantric cult in India, situated in the north eastern state of Assam, atop the Nilachal Hill. It is one of the 108 Sakti Peethas of Goddesses Durga.

Kalighat

Kalighat is an important pilgrimage for tantrics in Kolkata (Calcutta) many sacrificial ritual are completed before the Kali and a good number tantrics take part in rituals that are performed.

Bisnupur

In the district of Bankura of West Bengal is place for Tantrism. Intent on worshipping of Goddess "Manasa". Bisnupur is also an ancient well known cultural and craft centre.

---

[1] Siva Mahapurana - Uma Samahita, Ch. LX1, P-19.

Bhubneswara

The vaital temple belonging to circa 8th cen. A.D. is one of the representative powerful Tantric centre.

Inside the temple image of Chamunda (Kali) bearing a necklace of skulls with a corps at her feet, is worshipped by Tantrics, sitting at the feet of the Kali find dimly lit interior of the temple an ideal place for absorbing age old currents of power that emanate from this spot.

Eklingi

The four faced Saiv image carved in black marble stone inside the Siva temple near udaipur in Rajasthan. The temple belong to circa 8 th century A.D.. Tantric rituals are performed in the temple complex though out the year.

Balaji

Balaji is one of the most interesting and popular centres of Tantrics rituals performed by the worshippers, situated near Bharatpur (Rajasthan) Apart from the worshippers, common visitors visiting the temple leaves one with an eeric feeling .

Yogini temples

The yogini cult has its origin in the simple tribal folk tradition of India, during circa 7th- 8th century A.D. in Conjunction with the "Sakta-Tantric" form meaning the worship of Mother Goddess combined with certain magical rituals.

According to some later inscriptions found in certain yogini temples further indicate that the cult was practiced even the 16th century A.D.

Nothing is known about when yogini cult bowed out of limelight and its temples meant of Tantric rituals were abandoned, perhaps this is because of rising power of Brahmanical tradition. If we were to look for the origin of Yoginis, we must turn to the simple village cult and to the gramdevis the local village goddesses.

In the village of India, especially in Orissa, these are the favored deities Each gram devi is denoted as Ramchandi, Shyamkali, Harachands Tarini, Viraja, Bhagvati, Durgamata, Sarala, Bhadra Kali Kamakhya, Bhavani, Mangala etc. Precides over the welfare of the village.

These village goddesses seem to have been gradually transformed and consolidated, thus forming sixty four (Chausath Yogini) some times sixty eight and somtimes forty two, acquiring there by a totally different character.

It was tantrism that elevated these local deities and gave them new form of vigar as a group of goddesses who could bestow magical powers with a view to the destruction of enemies.

The remains of Yogini temples in various parts of the country viz. Chausath yogini temple at Bheraghat, Khajuraho (M.P.) Mirzapur (Uttara Pradesh), Orissa, (Hirapur) Tamil Nadu etc, Clearly indicate that the exponents and followers of this esoteric cult made viorous attempts to popularize it and this cult was of impelling and vital significance from circa 9th to 12th century A.D.

The Legonds

The legends behind this is that in the ancient scriptures, often yoginis are depicted as consorts of Yogis and like their male compeniens practiced Yoga (meditation) to gain mastery over science and acquire magical power "Kaula Marga" a tantric form of worship further includes yoginis of different categories in its cakra (circle) associated with lord Siva, discussed in preceding pages.

Concept of Vajrayana Buddhism

So far we have discussed about the tantric rituals performed by the Tantric worshipper of yogini as a form of "Devi" the supreme goddess of the "Sakta". The vajrayan or the Tantric form of Buddhism which evolved agaist the principles of Hinyan and Mahayan Buddhism preached by the Buddha himself, had laid great emphasis on the therory of emancipation. The preachers of Vajrayana Buddhism redefined "Nirvana" (liberation) as "Sunya" (Void) Vijnana and Mahasukha (extreme pleasure) that could be achieved by embracing a women. In this way this newly restructured nirvan, women were designated as "Sakti" and their union with "Sadhak" came to be know as a Yoga".

Further, vajrayana Buddhists were empowered to violate laws, kill human beings and seduce women. They propounded acommon slogan- identical actions by which mortals struggling for hundreds of billions of cycles could liberate the "yogin" (the Enlightened Man).

4

HAND POSES, ORNAMENTS, DRAPERY ASANAS, STANDING, SITTING, SAYANA, DANCING AND BHANGA, POSTURES OF ANCIENT ICONS

In the present context it is to be pointout here the sculptural hoard of central India, from the earliest times to the medieval period we see the art creation, the cannons of Silpasastras must be understood for a better reference of Icons to the different attitudes, poses ad gestures. These are not the result of single period but are the adaptation of different intellectual processes which take a superb shape in golden age of Gupta period.

It may be refered that a detailed account has been given in hand poses[1] which are depected in the Icons of deities and attendants of various sects of Hindu divinities.

The bhusparsa or Bhumisparsa pose in which the left hand rests on the lap and palm outward and the right hand with palm inward touches the seat below, as seen in Buddhist iconography.

---

[1] Fig. 7, 8.

In this pose Buddha is shown, calling the mother earth as his witness for testifying to his right to sit on the Vajrasana and the Bodhi tree, which was challenged by mara Just prior to his enlightenment.

The other hand poses of Buddha are Dharma Cakra pravartana and Bhusparsa Mudra, evolved during Mahayan Iconography.

Another hand poses of Dhyani Buddha may be depicted as Virocana and Aksobhya respeclively.

It is curious to note that with regard to the "Ornamentations" of Icons of different sects from the earliest times, the worshippers of image were very fond of displaying ornaments in the images of their gods and goddessess.

The various parts of the body viz: the head, the ears, the nose and neck, the breasts, the upper and lower arms, the palm, the fingers, the torso, the waist, the hip, the ankles, the feet had their various appropriate ornaments. so far as the Buddhism and Jainism is concerned, they were no doubt free from this peculiar feature, but the ornaments which could not be shown on their body, but they were seen depicted with great zeal on the images of Boddhisattavas, and Sasandevatas respectively. Even the very images of Buddha himself of the medieval period, in eastern India, were adorned with the jewelled crown (kirita) and elaborately designed torque.[1]

Such ornaments have also been found displayed in the images unearthed in Indus valley civilization.

The ornaments of God, displayed with Kirita-mukuta, specially appropriate for Narayan, according to the Mansara is a conical cap sometimes endingin an ornamental top carrying a central pointed

[1] Coomarswamy - J.R. A.S. 1928, P-837

Knob.[1] Such type of head gear was also used by Surya and Kubera. Varah Mihira describes Vishnuvas Kundalakiritadhari, Ravi should be Mukatdari Kuber should be vama kiriti the kirita should be placed slantingly on the left side of the head[2]

The goddess bears. patra kundalas, kantha hara, beaded garland, armlets, bracelets kangana, Nupura and mekhala, she also bear sari shown with many folds and uttariya.

In case of umas ornments, she bears chakrakundala, kanthahara, ekabali, hara, kutisutra, uruddam and pajebs on the legs.

The hara was a simple string of beads hanging down up to the breasts with different curves engraved beautifully. It consists of single, double, triple or even as many as five strings according the status of the wearer. Icons of parmara period are shown bearing two or more stringed haras which flow over the protrude breasts, seen in the images of Central Museum Indore. Likewise in Gwalior Museum images are shown with display of three stringed haras and pendants.

In Gupta age there is a rare use of katisutra is a note worthy feature of the Icons.

During the period ranging from circa 9th century A.D. to 12th century A.D. The Gods and Goddessess are vehemently ornamented with heavy Jewellary, which also exhibit more than half a dozen distinct designs of each type of ornament is a typical feature of the age.

The keyuras (armlets) are inseparable and essential part of jwellery for both male and female. In the Gupta period keyuras used were either plain or in round nature like a big bangle as depicted in the image of candella period viz; Khajuraho Temples.

---

[1] T.A.G. Rao - Uttarakamikagama Vol I P-27-28

[2] Brhatsamhita - Chap 57, V.V.32 P- 57

Apart from this valayas, nupuras and bangles are important ornaments, worn on each wrist. The design of the nupuras has either small bell shaped trinkets put together in chain or circular trinkets.

The great success achieved by the Indian artists/silpis is the representation and treatment of drapery. In the case of male imges the loin cloth (dhoti) whose folds are very tastefully arranged in parallel rows as seen in early and medieval period including a long scarf thrown loosely on the upper part of the body.

The Maurya and Sunga period and in later age the excess of long loin cloth is gathered together and shown hanging in a long tapering fold or folds in front, this feature is common in both male and female Icons (The image of parkhan yaksa and yaksi of Ḅesnagar are good example of such pattern of drapery.

The modern Jacket-like garment (angiya, angrakha) being nowher present. The diaphanousness (the transparency) of the drapery on the Buddha Icons of Sarnath and after ward is very effectively suggested by the silpis, and it certainly does not testify to their inability in indicating garments.

It is the printout here that Mathura yaksinis who appear to be nude or just about to divist themselves of their garments, these yaksinis are not depicted nude but are presented by the artists as clothed in most transparent of garments. or the nude female figures in the medieval art of Orissa and central India emphasise the carnal character of nackedness.

The representation of transparency carving work in stone by the silpis of India is a great tribute and honour to them.

In the Vaisnava cult, it was regarded as the religion which commands a high position in the society. The Icons of Vishu may be classified into three broad heads, viz; Sthanaka (Standing), asana (seated) and sayana (recumbent), in the vaikhasagama text. The Icons of other subordinate gods and their attendants are represented in one or other of the first two attitudes the recumbent ones being very rare.

The images of several varieties that are witnessed in flying pose like vidyadharas and others.

The standing (Sthanak) images, may, however be catagorised into four different standing poses, and are called Sthana Kamurtis, they known as Bhangas I.e. "flexious or attitudes".

These images are :- Sambhanga, or sampada, abhanga, tribhanga and atibhanga.

It is to point out here that Jain Tirthankaras whose hands also hang straight down by their sides without showing the least bend in them (kayotsarga).

The Buddhist and Brahmanical divinities when they are shown in this attitude, usually are found in various disposition of their hands. The Abhanga is that form of standing pose, in which the plumb line or the centre line from the crown of head to a point midway between the heels, passes slighly to the right of the naval. This representation is found in most of Icons of different sects.

Reference may be made in respect of the Icons, to the "Alidha" and pratyalidha poses in which some standing images are carved in relief by the silpis.

The tribhang[1] pose has been described by A.N. Tagore as one in which the centre line passes through the left (or right) pupil, the middle of the chest, the left (or right) of the navel, down to the heels. The lower limbs, from the hips to the feet are displaced to the right (or left) of the Icon, the trunk between the hips and neck, to the left (right)

[1] J.N. Banerjea- The development of Hindu Iconography New Delhi. 1974, P.266.

while the head leans towards the right (or left) It is to be noted that the number of bends in the Icon is three.

The Atibhang has been rarely represented in Indian art and is used in dynamic action of the divinity, several ugra forms of Siva and Sakta deities and various krodha devatas and in vajrayan Buddhism this Ati bhanga form is Visualised.

The Ahirbudhnya - Samhita (ch-30), about eleven asanas viz; Cakra, Padma, Kurma, Mayura, Kaik Kuta, Vira, Swastika, Bhadra, Simha, Mukta, and Gomukha.

The asana mean a seat or even pedestal, while the word pitha is seldom used, white padmapitha would indicate the lotus seat on which the deity is seated. According to T.A. Gopinath Rao, there are five kinds of asanas as metioned in Superbhedagama Viz; Anantasana, Simhasana, Yogasana, Padmasana, and Vimlasana, respectively.

Sayana or fully recumbent images of Hindu divinities are extremely rare. Jalasayin and vatpatrasayan aspect of Visnu, ideologically similar to sesasayana of Visnu.

The Anantasayana mutri of Visnu situated in one of the side of niches of the Deograh temple of Gupta period is one of the finest representation of its own kind of this motif in Indian art. likewise the Mahaparinirvana murti of Buddha is a recumbant image belonging to Buddhist pantheon.

According to Natya Sastras and agamas, different rhythms and poses of dance are described in details Siva is supposed to be the great dancer and musician in the universes, hence he is called Natraja. These two activities were also associated with Saktis also. An interesting images of Kali, which was recovered from patales wara temple (shahdol) is a rare representation of dance. It is at present displayed in Birla Museum Bhopal.

5

CONCLUSION

Since the dawn of human evolution on the earth crust and with the expansion and development of cultural activities, in the society of mankind, the ape man's civilization spotted by cultural remains of ancient times.

This may be marked as the beginning of the new era for the sequential evolution of man in stages.

The civilization of early man limitted to dense forests, who started his home land there and living on vegetal food.

After a long span of time, when the cranial capacity increased to maximum of cromagnon 1600 c.c. and 1300 to 1600 cc. of Homocepian man.

Habilis man was the first inventer of tool making. They lived in caves by nature they were omnivorous and also show cannibalism i.e. at the time of paucity of food for them in the forest, then they eat the flesh of members of their own species too. It includes Javaman, Pekingman, and Heidel berg man.

In preceding pages we have discussed about human development with his cranial capacity.

The human body is divided into head, neck, torso (Trunk) and limbs. The Trunk is subdivided into chest or thorax and belly or obdomen.

In standing (Sthanak) Posture, it is called "Sama Bhanga" posture in details it was dealt in precceding pages), an upright position, the upper limbs hanging by the sides and the palms of the hands directed forwards. This is the anatomical position.

So far as the ancient Icons are concerned these have been fashioned by the skilled silpis under various royal dynasties, the edges of plane of torso is confirmed into various geometrical patterns, discussed, comparing with the Icons of different sects, illustrated in figures and plates respectively.

In preceding pages an attempt has been made for the first time to examine critically the genesis of "Geometrical patterns" of ancient Icons of different sects of various dynasties of ancient India.

From the close study of ancient Icons of different sects, those in-situ, and displayed and preserved in various Museum of India, in general and particular in central India, have been brought together. A comprehensive, photography has been done and Icons and problems have been critically discussed in the present text.

In chapter-2 deals with Ancient Icons, Iconographical features of ancient Icons under different trends of art of India have been discussed beginning with 3rd and 4th millenia. B.C. beginning with the following sects :-

Yaksa Cult

Salbhanji Kas - Nayikas, Abhisarikas, Sursandaris.

Mauryan - Sungas - Satvahnas (Buddhist art)

Kusana- period (circa 2nd century A.D.)
Icons of Gupta age.
Pantheon of Lakulisha
Icons of Pratihara age
Icons of Parmara age
Icons of Kalcuri age
Icons of Candella age
Icons of Kachchapaghata age

Chapter-3 is devoted to the icon-worship, Tantirc cult and tantric centres of ancient India.

The most noteworthy features of Iconographic representation of worship is Icon. The Icons are made with the basic aim of being worshiped. Image worship is an out come of devotional sentiments from inner self.

Linga worship has been of wide prevalence in the ancient world we meet with the vestiges of it in India.

Siva is worshiped in the symbol of "Linga" and also in the anthropomorphic form.

Under defferent trends of art and Iconography symbolic worship was in vogue during Himyana phase of worship. Later on during Mahayana phase Buddha was worshipped in Icon form.

Sun worship was prevelent in ancient India in form of images.

Like Saiva, Vaisnava cult under the Brahmanical religion possessed a commanding position.

The worship of Visnu got a high position in the society.

In the field of Iconography as well as religious literature, indicates the terrible form of Siva was utilized by Tanstrist.

In the medieval period Tantrism associated with Brahmanical Hindaism as well as mahayanas or Vajrayan form of Buddhism attained full development in India.

Likewise during candella dynasty, Buddhism and Tantrism was prevelent and many of the magnificent Jaina and Buddhist temple are still witnessing the Icons of Buddha and Buddhist goddess Tara, with the existence of Tantric cult.

Interestingly is the fact that Khajuraho was one. of the main Kapalik centres where "Rati cakra Mahotrava" was the main function of kapalikas, where in the erotic images reflect the hold of Kaul and Kapalika sects here.

The well known "panchamkar" of Kaulas gained more popularity in those days.

Central India including malwa was important regions where Tantric practices were prevelent since ancient times specially in "Daksina-Kosala region.

The important Tantric centres of ancient India are

Kamakhya

Kalighat

Bhubneswara

Eklingi

Balaji

Apart from the above, the yogini cult has its origin in the simple tribal folk tradition. of India, during circa 7-8th century A.D. in conjunction with the "Sakta-Tantric" form, meaning the worship of Mother goddess conbimed with certain magical rituals.

A comprehensive study of Icons, discussed in the preceding chapter we must not over look the importance of Hand poses, ornaments drapery Asanas, Standing, sitting, Sayana, dancing and Bhanga postures of ancient Icons these have been our main aim was to focus light on them.

We have confirmed that of the geometrical pattern of Torso of Icons was considered to be the best of Iconography of ancient India.

Thus the present work is based on comprehensive field work and hence may be claimed as an indigeneous approach to discuss the subject critically.

It is expected that the present work would be useful for scholars concerned and common mass.

SELECT BIBLIOGRAPHY

Sanskrit Text

Ṛg Veda - F. Maxmullar Poona 1890-92

Atharva Veda - Visvesarananda, Vedic Research Institute, Hoshiyarpur, 1962

Astadhyayi - (Panini) (Ed) S.C. Basu, Allahabad 1929

Bhagavt- Puran - Saraswati Press, Calcutta, 1882

Vaman Puran - Venkateswar Press, Bombay

Ramayan - M.M. Datta, Culcutta, 1982-94

Silpa-Sastra

Aprajitprcha - (Bhuwan Deva) (Ed) P.A. Mankad Gaikwad oriental series No CXIV, Baroda, 1950

Rupamandana - (Mandana), Balram Shrivastav, Motilal Banarsidas, Varanasi, Samvat 2021.

Samarangana Sutradhara - (Bhoj) (Ed) T.G. Shastri

MODERN WORK

Acharya P.K. - Encyclopedia of Hindu Architecture Reprint, Delhi 1974

Agrawal P.K. - Pracina Bharatiya Kala Evam Vastu Varansi 2002

Ali Rahman - Art and Architecture of the Kalcuris Delhi 1987

Agarwala Urmila - Khajuraho Sculptures and their significance, Delhi, 1964

Agarwala V.S. - Indian art Varanasi, 1965
Matsya Purana- A study Varanasi, 1963
Vamana Purana- A study, Varanasi, 1964
Gupta art, Varanasi, 1977

Awasthi Ramashrya - Khajuraho Ki Deva Pratimayen, Agra, 1967

Agarwala R.A. - History of art and architecture of Jaisalmer, Delhi, 1974

Banarjea J.N. - Development of Hindu Iconography Calcutta, 1956

B. Rolend - Art and architecture of India, Cambridge, 1933

Bajpai K.D. - Madhya Pradesh Sculptures through the age, Marg Vol. XXVI, 1933.

Bhandarkar D.R. - Ashoka, calcutta, 1955

Bhatia P. - The Parmaras, New Delhi, 1970

Bhattacharya P.K. - The Indian Mother Goddess, Delhi, 1979

Brown P. - Indian Architecture (Buddhist, Hindu and Jain), Bombay, 1944

Bachoffer L. - Early Indian sculpture, Paris, 1929

Bhandarkar R.G. - Vaisnavism, Saivism and minor religious system, varanasi, 1965

Biswas T.K. - Gupta Sculptures, Delhi, 1985

Chakravarty C. - The Tantras, Studies on their Religion and literature, Calcutta, 1963

Chandra Promod - Stone Sculptures in Allahabad Museum, Poona, 1970

Cunningham A. - Stupa of Bharhut (Second Ed.) Varanasi, 1962
Bhilsa Tope (Reprint) Varanasi, 1962

Chakravarty K.K - Gwalior Fort, Delhi, 1984

Deva K - Temples of North India, New Delhi, 1963

Dwivedi S.K. - Temple Sculptures of India, New Delhi, 1991

Dikshit S.K. - A Guide to State Museum Dhubela Poona, 1955-57
A Guide to Gwalior Museum, 1962

Gupta R.S. - Iconography of Hindu, Buddhist and Jain, Bombay, 1972

Garde M.B. - Archaeology in Gwalior State Gwalior, 1934

Ganguly D.C. - History of Parmaras Dynasty, Dacca, 1955

Khare Harle, Ganesha Hari - Indian Sculptures, Delhi, 1961

Kala S.C. - Sculptures in the Allahabad Museum

Kumar P. - Sakti Cult in Ancient India, Varanasi, 1974

Misra I. - Pratima Vijnana, Bhopal, 1972

Patil D.R. - Cultural Heritage of Mdhya Bharat, Gwalior, 1952

Pagne E.A. - The Sakta, Oxford University Press, 1933

Rao T.A.G. - Elements of Hindu Iconography, 2 vols Delhi, 1968

Sahai B. - Iconography of Hindu, Buddhist and Jain deities, Delhi, 1973

Saraswati S.K. - A Survey of Indian Sculpture, Calcutta, 1957.

Singh A.P. - Conservation and Museum Technique Delhi, 1987
Fort and fortification of India Delhi, 1987 Second (Ed.) Delhi, 1993
Defensive art of India, Delhi, 1990

Monuments of Orchha, Delhi, 1991
Monuments of Mandu, Delhi, 1994
Concept of Environment in art and architecture, Delhi, 2003
Monuments a Vision of Harmony Delhi, 2009

Sharma R.K. - The Temple of Chausatha yogini at Bheraghat, Delhi, 1978
Parmara Art, Delhi, 1979

Shastri R.P.S. - Sakti Tantra Darsan, Nagda, 1977

Sircar D.C. - Sakta Pitha, Calcutta, 1968
Sakti cult and Tara, Calcutta, 1967

Shrivastava- V.C. - Sunworship in Ancient India, Allahabad, 1972

Tripathi K.K. - Archacology of Vidisha Region, Delhi, 2002

Gazetteers

The central India state Guzetteers series Bhopal District Gazeteer, Vidisha, Bhopal 1979. Gwalior State Gazetteer, Gwalior, Bhopal.

INDEX

A

abdomen 21, 38
abhanga 89
acquafauna 39
Aditya 74
Ajanta caves 44
Alidha 89
amalgamation 64
Anantasayana mutri 90
aniconic form 29
Animal figures 58
anthropomorphic form 69, 71, 93
Apsaras 61
Ardhanariswara 71, 73
art for art sake 28
Ashapuri 53
Astadhyayi 36, 97
Atharveda 34
atibhanga 89
Atindra 75
avifauna 39

B

Bagh caves 43
Bana-Linga 69
benedictory verses 67, 75
Bhakti 29, 30, 43, 68
Bhakti cult 43
bhangas 64
bhangimas 64
Bhoga 28, 79
Bhoja 52
Bhoramdeo temple 62
Boddhisattavas 86
bodhi tree 41
Brahmanical Trinity 53

C

Cakra 41, 80, 86, 90
cedimandala 57
Chakra 73
chamardharni yaksi 40
chamunda 82
Chandreh 57
civilization 17, 24, 27, 68, 73, 86, 91
classical percepts 64
Cosmic Dance 72
costumes 49
cranial capacity 17, 91
cromagnon 17, 91
customs 58, 67

D

Dahalamandal 56
Daksina Murti 47
Dhanapati 34
Dhanga 60
Dhangadeva 60
Dharma 27, 31, 44, 86
Dikpalas 61
Divilingi Lakulisha 47
dress and drapery 40
Dubkunda 64
dvadasdita 73
Dvibhanga 38

E

erotic images 62, 78, 79, 94

F

fauna 39
female kapalin 81
feudalistic society 60
flexion 21, 22
flora 39
Floral designs 58
foliation 53
folk art 23, 31

G

Ganas 61
Gandhar 42, 69
Gandhar Style 42
Gandharvapuri 53
Gangeyadeva 57
Gathasaptasati 81
genesis 24, 30, 70, 92
Geometrical pattern designs 58
giagantic 61
gigantic 31, 32, 53, 54
Goddesses 49, 61, 62, 70, 81
Gods 34, 46, 49, 61, 62, 70, 72, 87
Golden age 44
Golkimath 57
Gopadri fort 63
Gupta age 43, 44, 54, 87, 93
Gurgi 57
Gurjara Partiharas 52
Gurjara Pratiharas 60

H

Hari-Hara 56, 73, 76
Hari- Harakka 73
Harsa 48, 60
Heidel berg man 18, 91
Hinglajagarh 48
Hinglajgarh 53, 54, 55, 56
Hinyana pantheon 39
Homo - sapiens sapiens 20
homocepian man 17
Homo sapiens futuralies 20

I

Icon 25, 40, 67, 75, 89, 90, 93
Iconic form 41, 42, 54, 69
Iconic worship 54
Image worship 67, 93
incarntion of Siva 47

J

Jaina monks 26
Jain Shasan devtas 61
Java man 18

K

ka-malapuspa 73
kachchapaghata dynasty 63
kalcuris of Ratanpur 57
Kalcuris of sarayupar 57
Kalcuris of Tripuri 57
Kamakhya temple 81
Kamikagama 69
kangana 61, 87
Katimekhala 40, 61
katisutra 87
Kaulkapalik 61
kausambi 33, 40
kayotsarga 89
Kirita-mukuta 86
Kirtivarman 60
Kundala 38, 61

L

Lakulisha 46, 47, 48
Linga puran vayupuran 47
Linga worship 68, 93

M

Mahaparinirvana murti 90
Mahayana 41, 70, 74, 77, 93
Mahishmati 56, 57
Manasa 81
manibhadra 35
mansara Suprabhedagmas 69
manusa linga 71
Matamayur 57
mekhala 87
mithuna 61
Monalisa 39
mother Goddess 68
mudras 44
murals 43, 44
mythology 68

N

Nagara-devata 35
Narvarman 52
Narwar 64
Natraja 71, 72, 90
Natraja form 72
Natya Sastras 90
Neanderthal 18, 19, 20
Neellohit 46
Nemavar 53
Nirvana 84
Nupura 87
nupura 61

O

Ominipotent 69
Omkar Mandhata 53
orthodox 67
oval face 58

P

padhavali 63
Padmanath temple 63
Padmasana 43, 90
padmasana 42, 47
padmavati 35
panchamkar 94
panchmukhi Mahadeva 72
parabolic 34
parkham yaksa 35
Parsva Devata 61
Passion 64

pasupathinath 72
Pasupati 28, 46
patra kundalas 87
peking man 18
phallic cult 68
Physiological 33
pitamah 28
postures 21, 22, 44, 49, 85, 95
Prabhamandala 49, 58
prathana slokas 67
pratyalidha 89
prehistoric period 46
pucker lines 44
puspa Kundala 38

R

Ramgarh 53
Rashrakutas 52
rati 61
ratichakra mahotsava 62
renunciation 31
rhythemic movement 22
rituals 28, 62, 67, 77, 78, 81, 82, 83, 84, 95
robust 31
rock shelter 46
Rupkara 25

S

Saila 25
sakyamuni 28
salbhanjika 36, 38, 41
Salil krida 41
Samabhanga 42, 61
sampada 89
samyak-sambhudda 28
Sandhara 53
Sasandevatas 86
Saumya 44, 62
Shardula 62
Shringar 49, 61
silpatexts 47
silpi 25
simple tribal 82, 94
Skhalit Vasna nayika 61
sohania 63
spiritualism 49, 61
squaresh 58
sthapati 25
sturdiness 44
Sukhasana 62
Sun temple Konark 62
Sur-Sundaris 61
sutradhara 25
Svambhuva lingas 69
Swarnapatra 73
Symbolic representation 39
symbolism 27

T

Tantric philosophy 70
tantric rituals 62, 84
Telika Mandir 49
terracotta image 33
The Gandhara School 44
The Mathura School 44
tribhanga 49, 89
Tridev 58
Trideva 59, 73, 75, 76

U

udyan krida 41
Ugra 62
unwieldy 57

V

Vaisnava cult 74
vajrayana 78, 84
vakatakas 57
Vakpati Raj 52
valayas 88
Vartula 73
Vatsala Nayika 61
Vedic culture 27
vedic literatre 67
vishnu 54
Vrsavahana murti 71
vyantara devatas 73

W

worship 25, 27, 28, 30, 34, 40, 41, 46, 49, 53, 54, 61, 67, 68, 69, 71, 72, 73, 74, 75, 76, 77, 80, 81, 82, 83, 93, 95

Y

yajna varah 54
Yaksa-Raj 34
yaksa yaksi 40
Yasovarman 60
Yoga 28, 79, 83, 84
yoga-Mudra 47
yogapatta 47
yogini-pithas 78

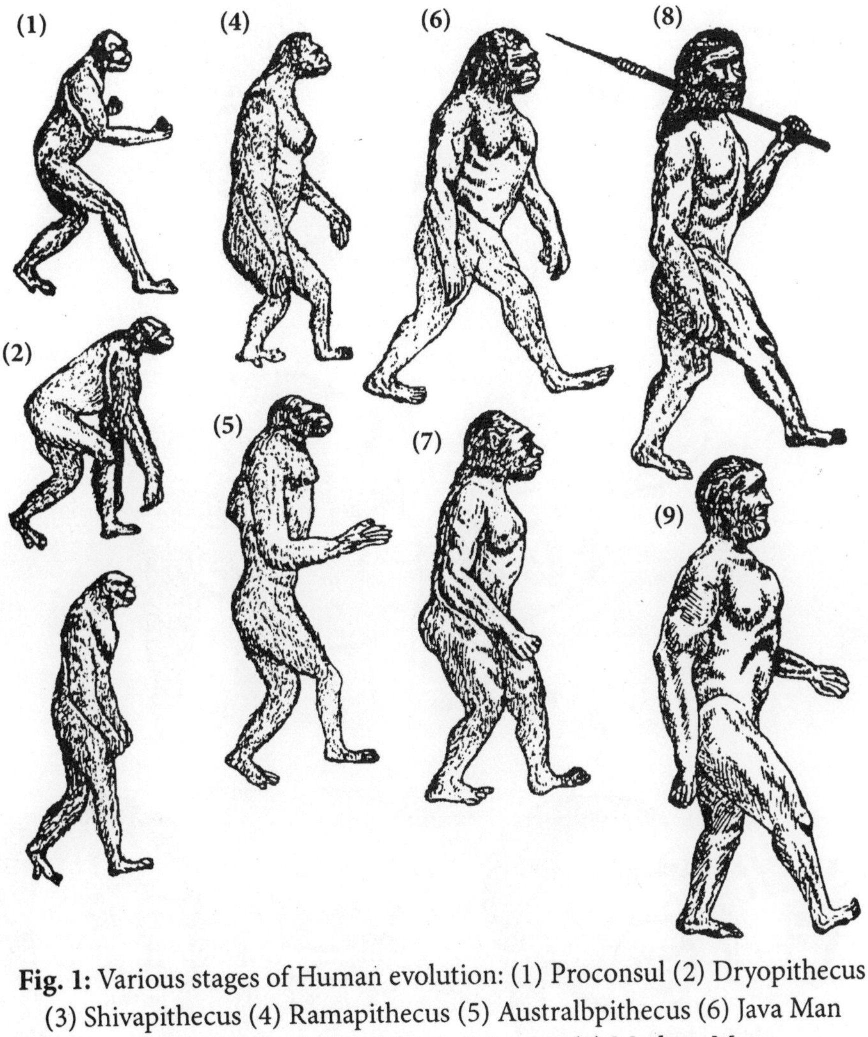

Fig. 1: Various stages of Human evolution: (1) Proconsul (2) Dryopithecus (3) Shivapithecus (4) Ramapithecus (5) Australbpithecus (6) Java Man (7) Neanderthal Man (8) Cro-Magnon (9) Modern Man

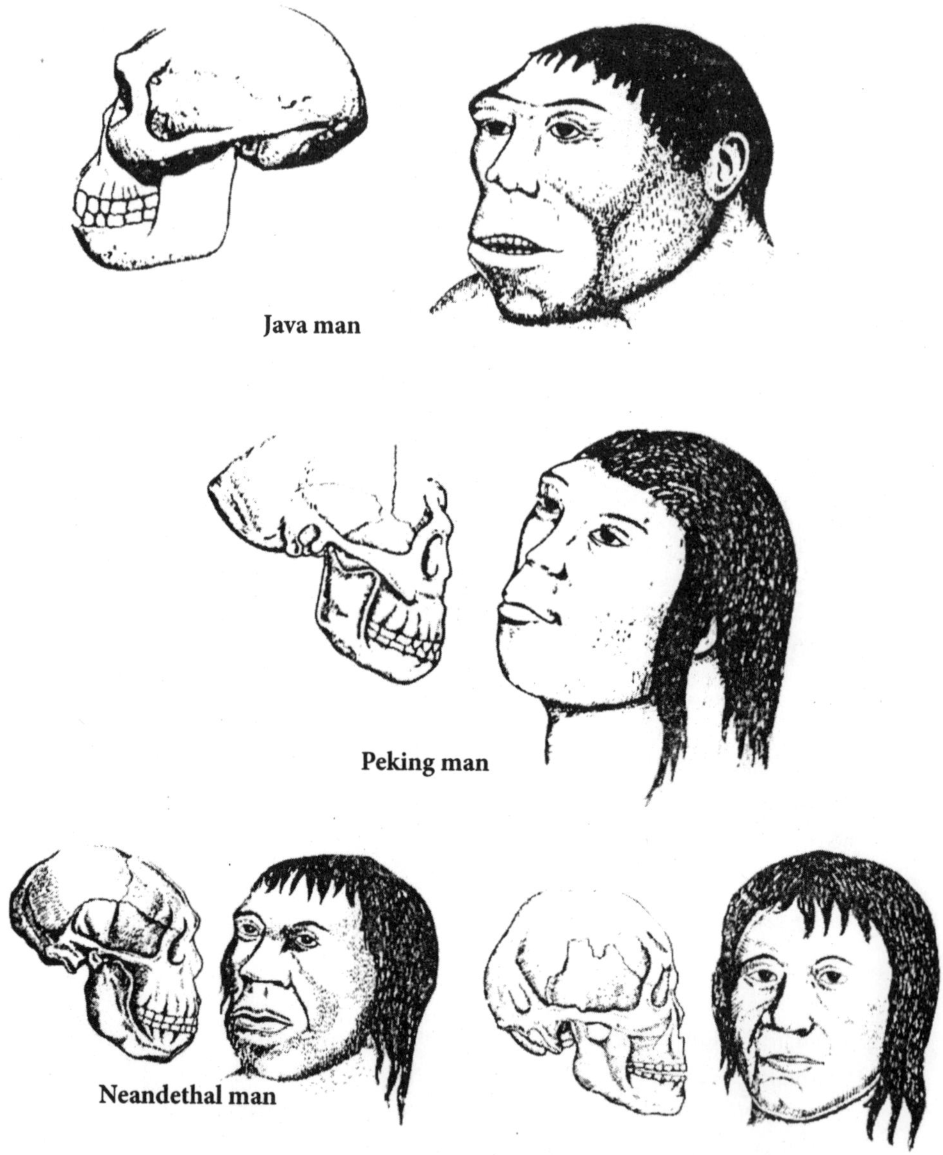

Fig. 2: Javaman, Pekingman, Neanderthalman, and Cromagnonman.

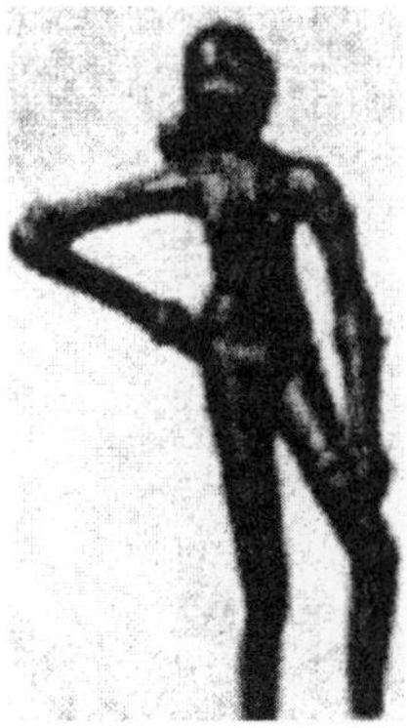

A. Dancing girl from Harappa

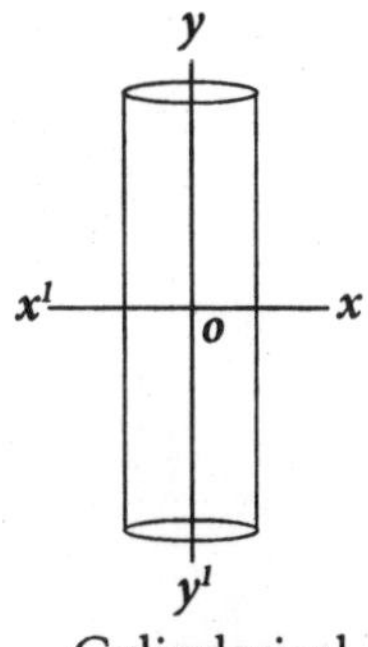

Cylinderical

B. Kuber yaksa from Besnagar (Vidisha)

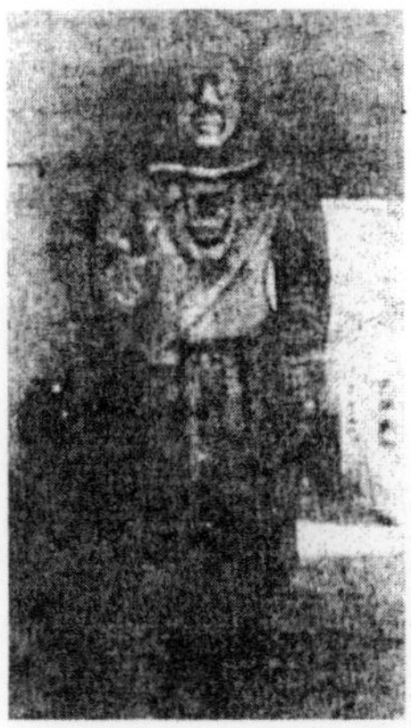

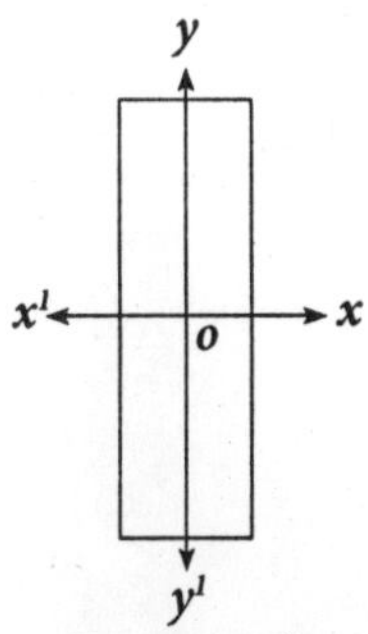

Rectangular

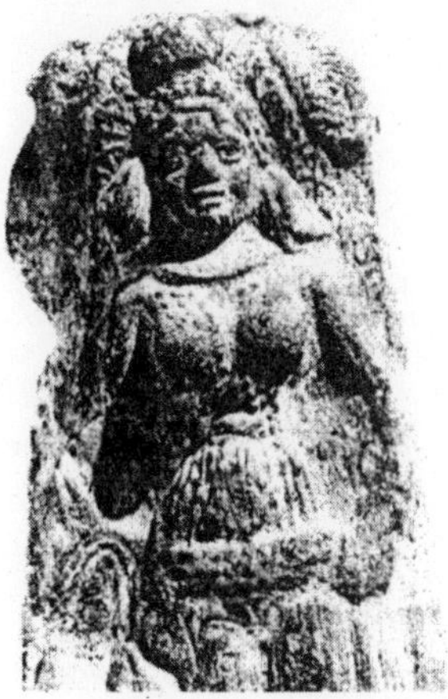

C. Yaksi from Ahichhatra (Allahabad)

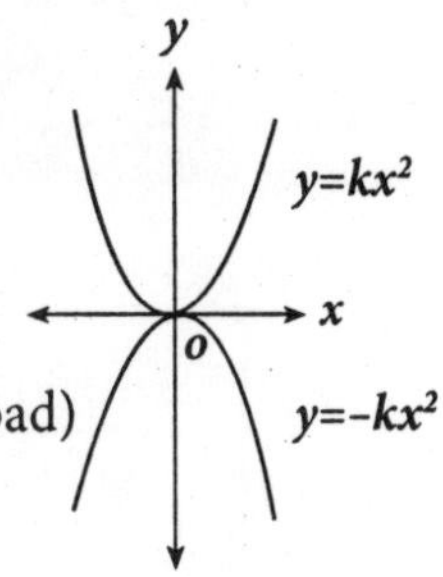

Parabola

Fig. 3: Geometrical patterns of Ancient Icons (Torso)
Indus valley civilization 3rd - 4th Millennia, B.C.

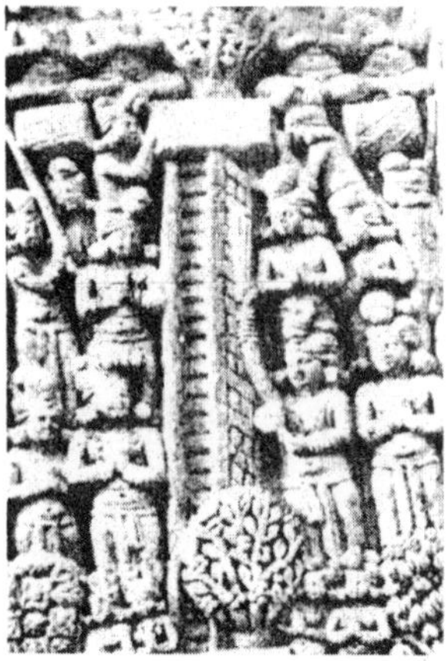

A. Torangate of Sanchi

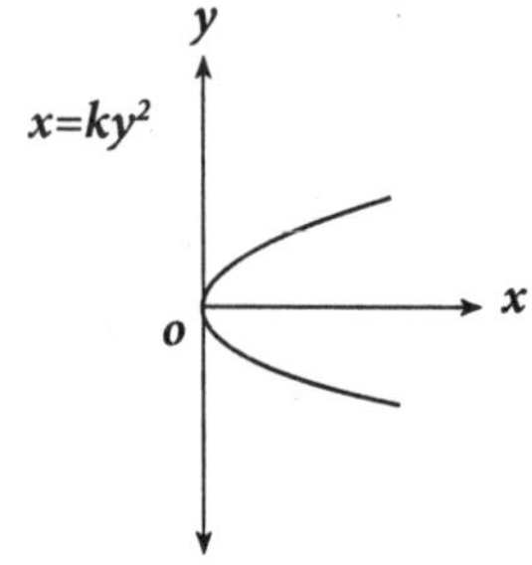

Paabola

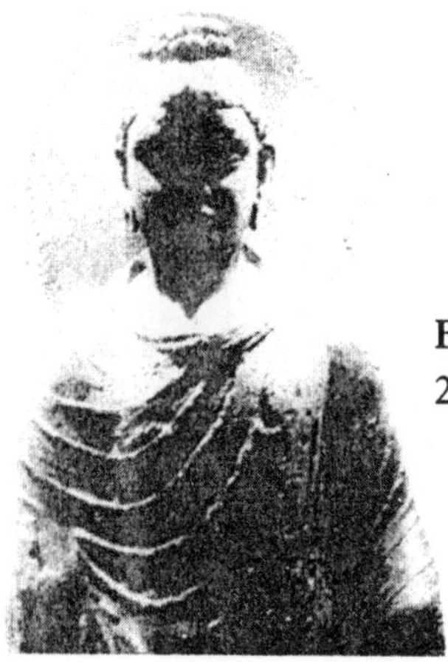

B. Kushana Period
2nd century A.D.

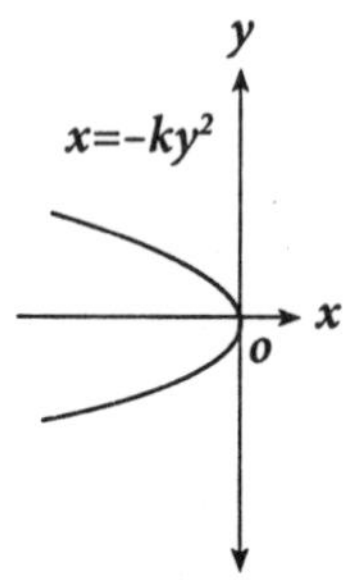

Paabola

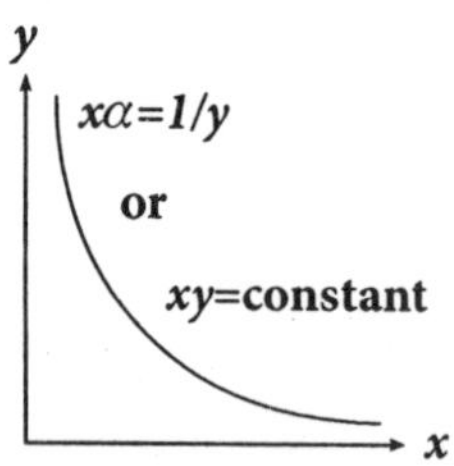

Hyperbola

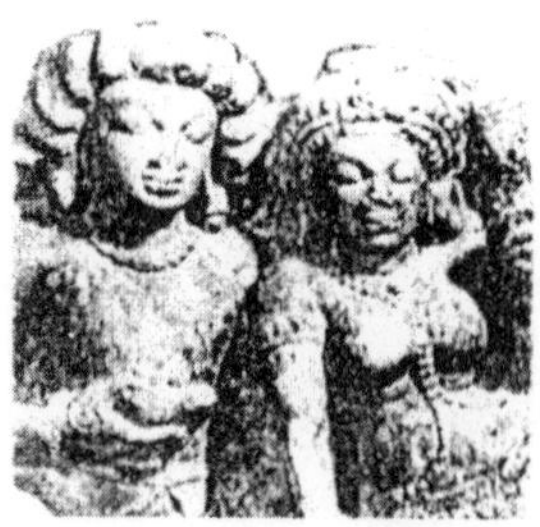

C. Gupta Period
4th-5th century A.D.

Fig. 4: Satvahana Period 1st century B.C.-1st century A.D.

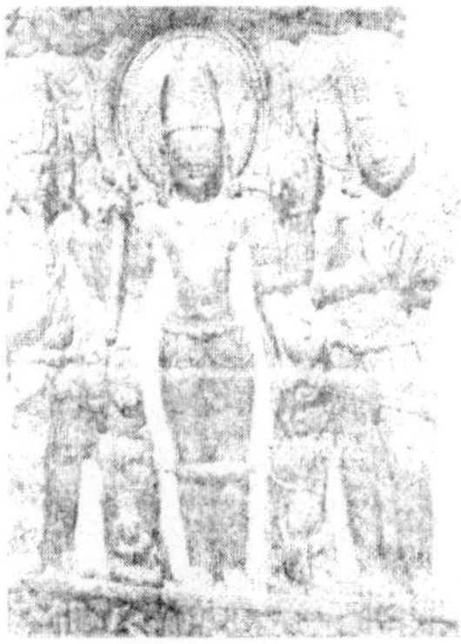

A. Kalcuri Period

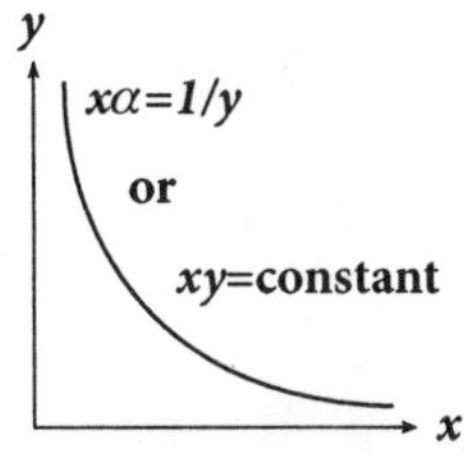

Hyperbola

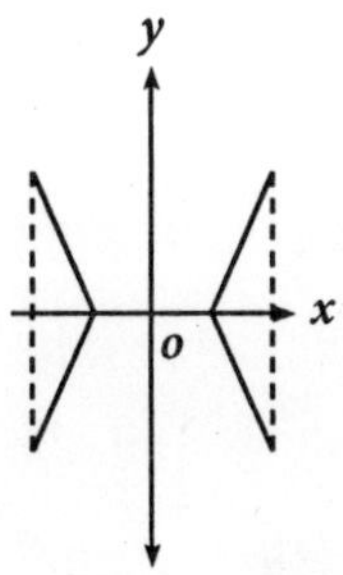

Bi-Triangular

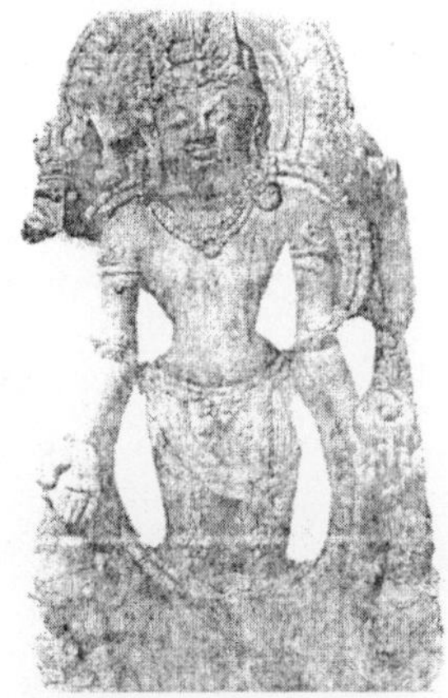

B. Pratihara Period

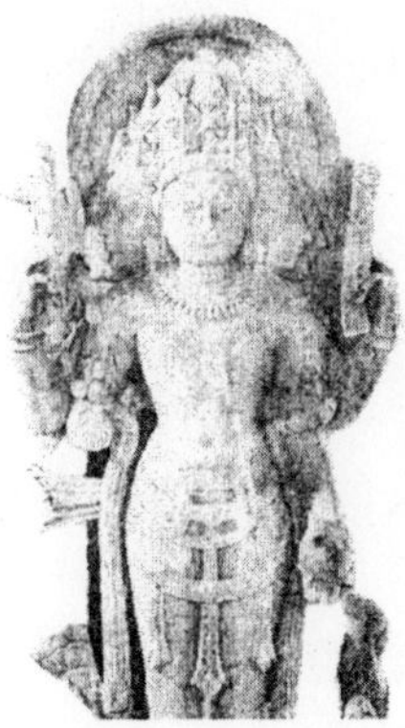

C. Parmara Period
10th Century A.D.
12th Century A.D.

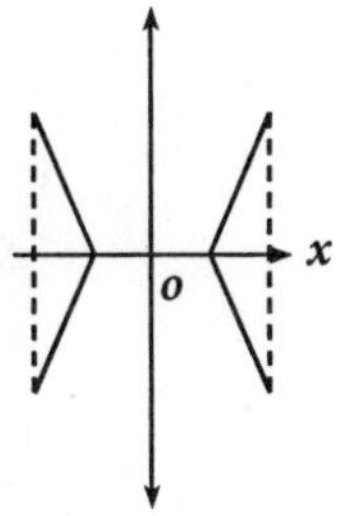

Bi-Triangular

Fig. 5: Kalcuri Period 6th century A.D. 11th century A.D.

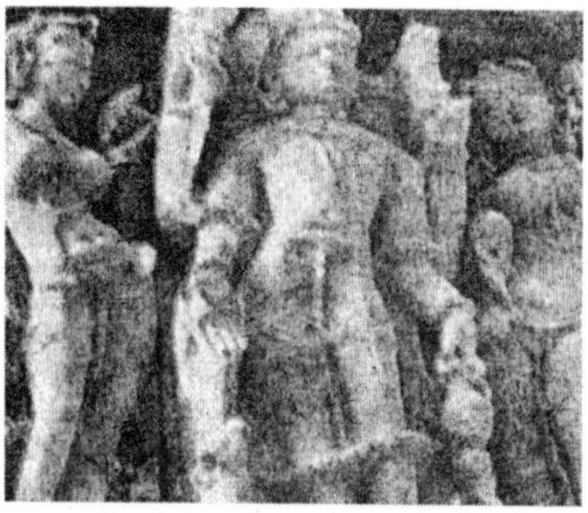

Fig. 6A: Candella Period
10th century A.D. - 12th century A.D.

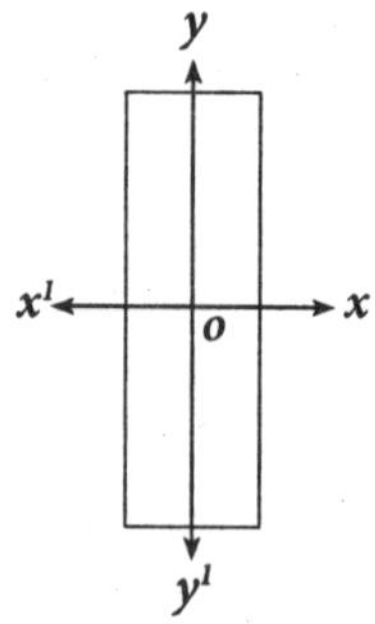

Trapezoid

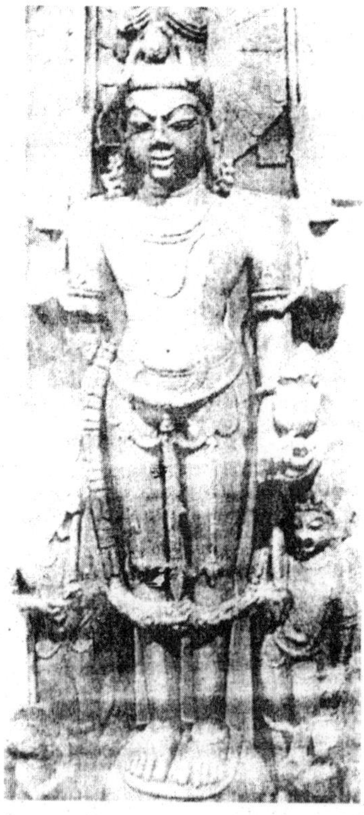

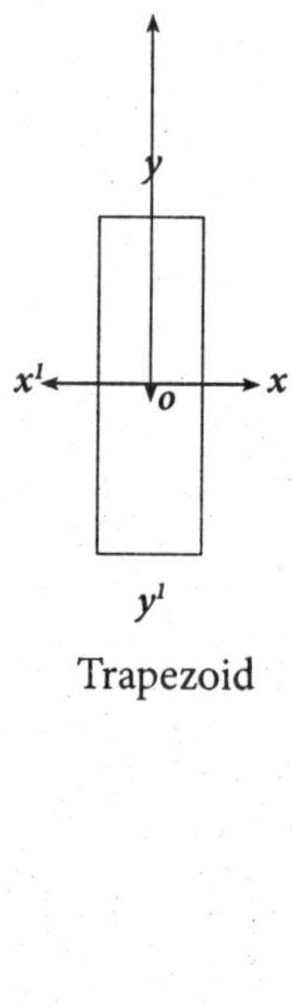

Trapezoid

Fig. 6B: Kachhapaghata Period - 10th century A.D. - 12th century A.D.

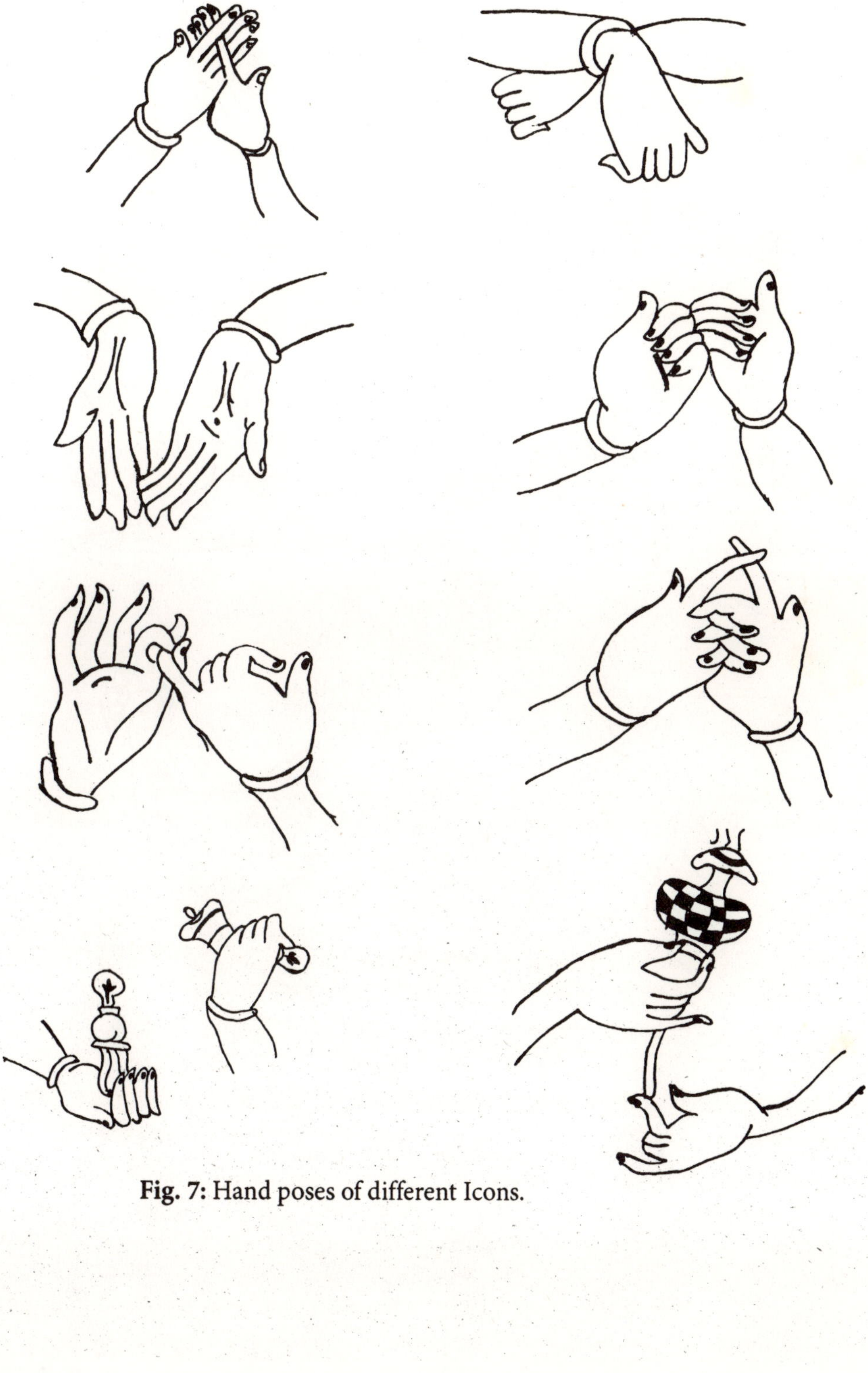

Fig. 7: Hand poses of different Icons.

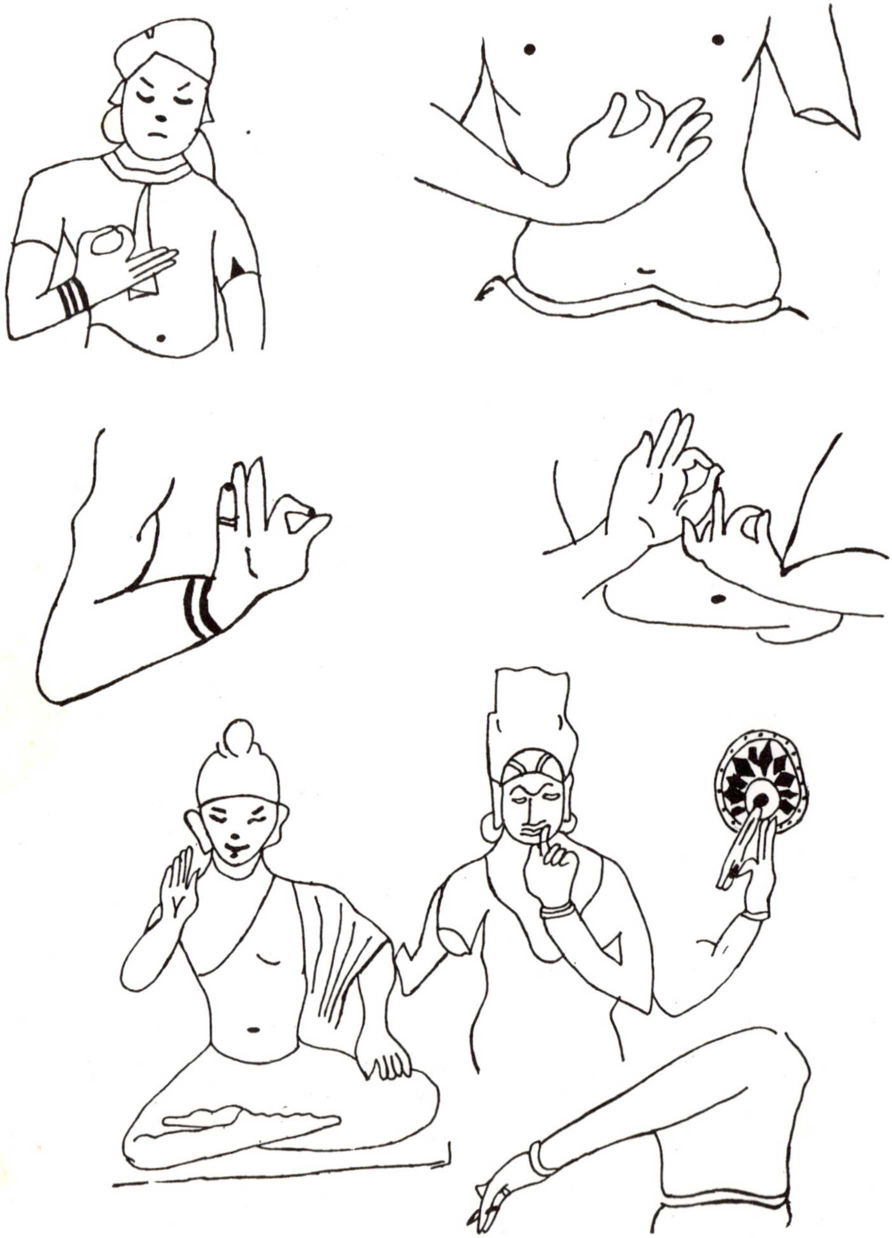

Fig. 8: Hand poses (Mudras) of different Icons.

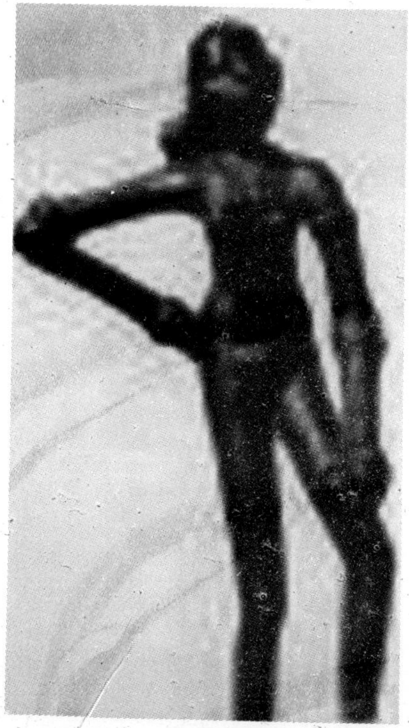

Pl. 1A: Dancing girl of Indus valley.

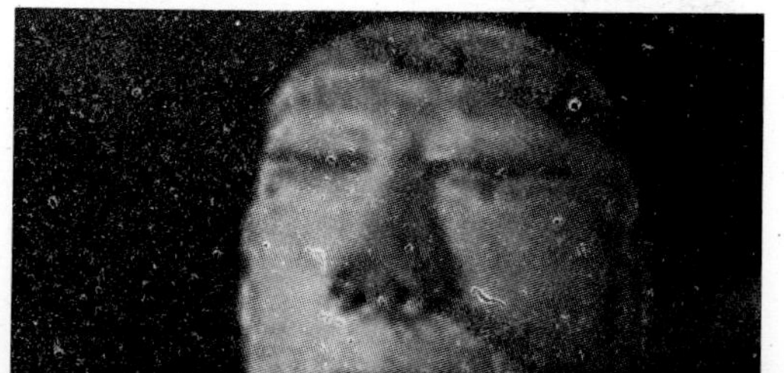

Pl. 1B: Icon of Priest of Indus valley.

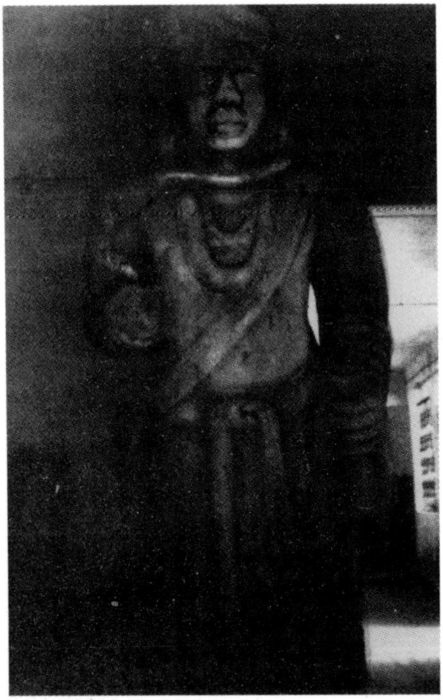

Pl. 2: Kuber yaksa from Besnagar Vidisha 2nd century B.C.

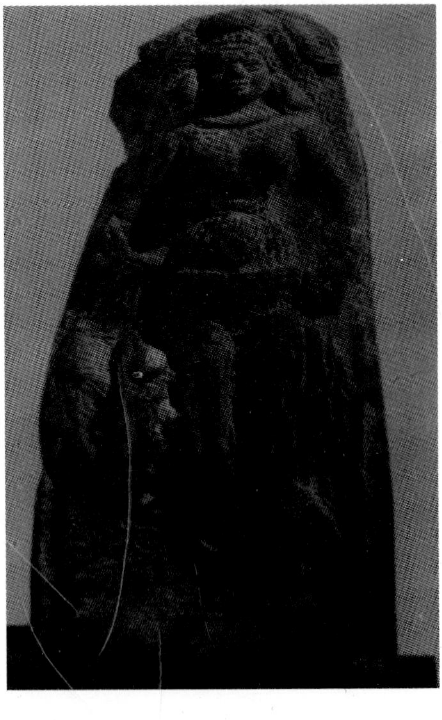

Pl. 3: Yaksi from Ahichhatra (Allahabad) Sunga period.

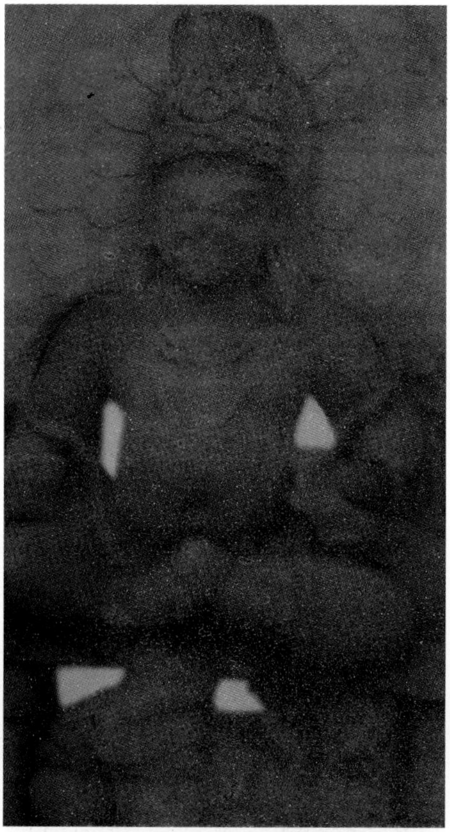

Pl. 4: Kuber Yaksa from Badoh, Vidisha 7-8th century A.D.

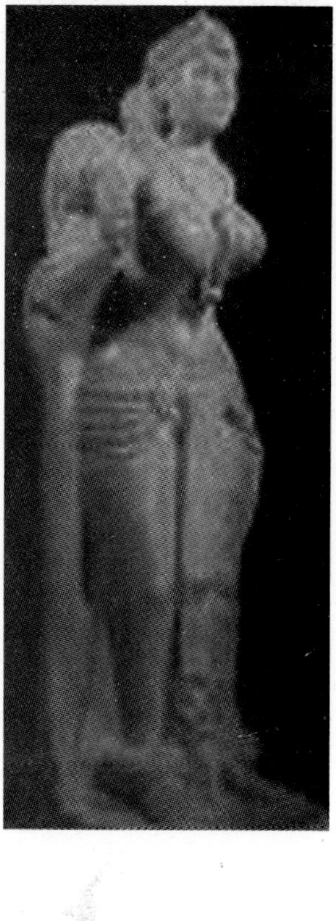

Pl. 5A: Chamar dharini yaksi, sunga period

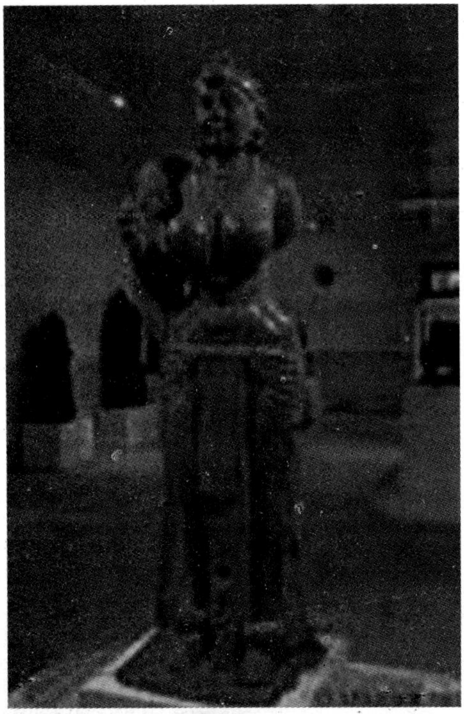

Pl. 5B: Yaksi of sunga period representing ornaments and drapery.

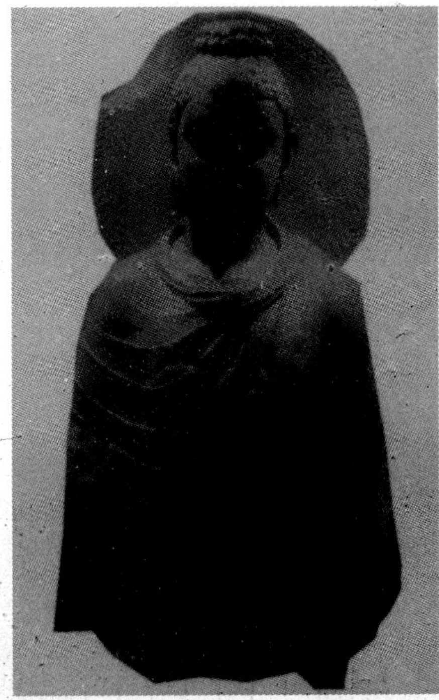

Pl. 6: Buddha Standing Kushana Period Gandhar Style

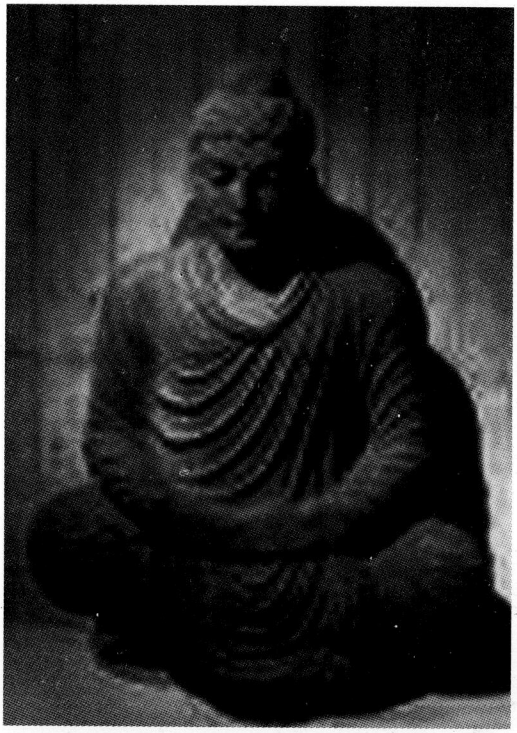

Pl. 7A: Dhyansta Buddha in asana (Seated) Kushana period, Gandhara Style.

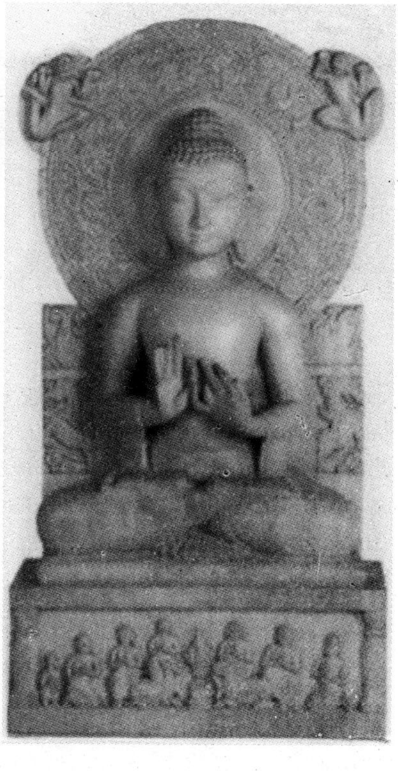

Pl. 7B: Budha seated in padmasana, preaching- Mudra, Kushana period, Mathura Style.

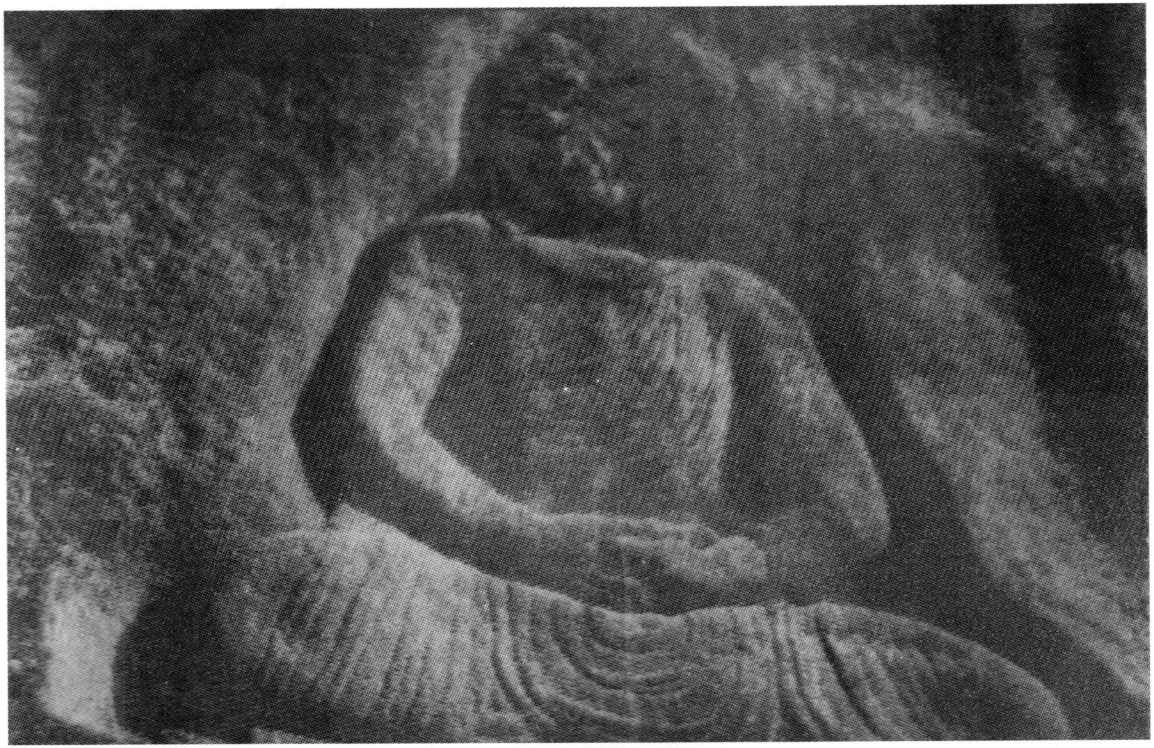

Pl. 8: Buddha seated in padmasana from swatvally Afghanistan Kushana period, Gandara style.

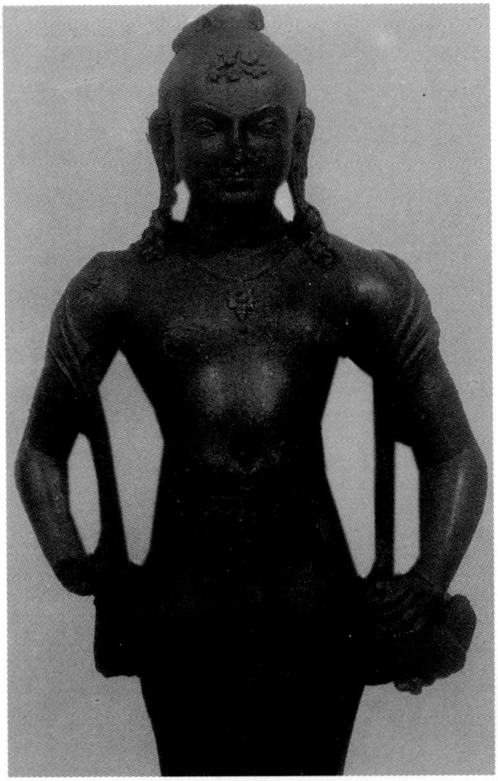

Pl. 9: Kumar Krtikeya, Gajendra Ghat, Mandsaur 4th- 5th century A.D.

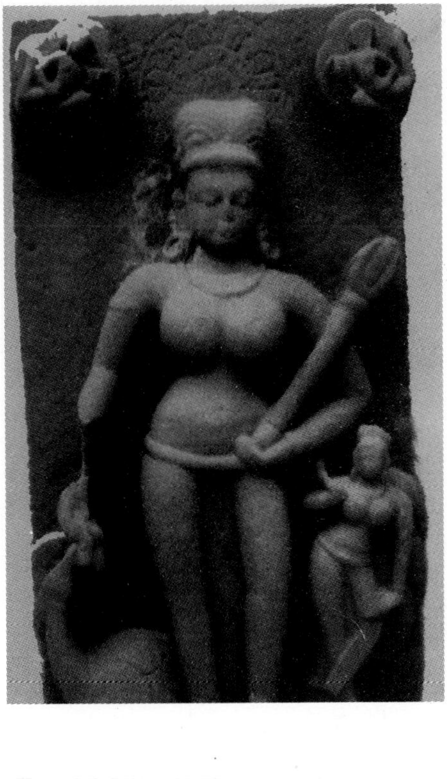

Pl. 10: Kaumari, Nachand, Panna 6th century A.D.

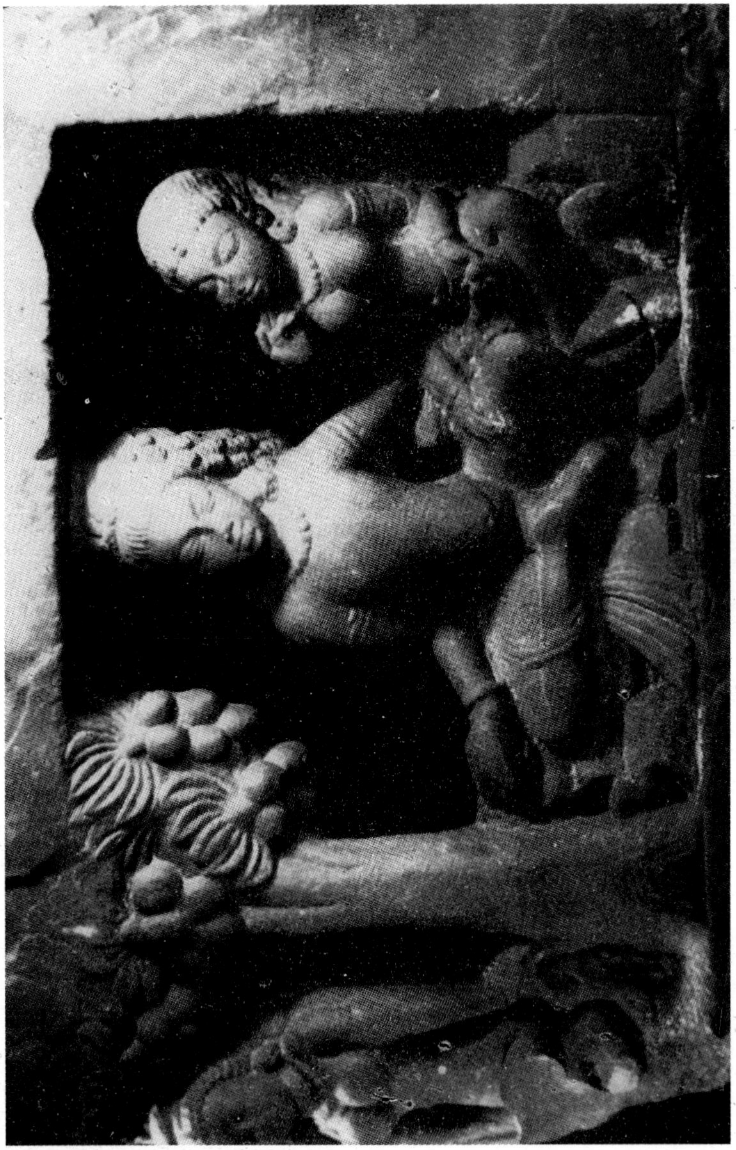

Pl. 11: Siva Parvati, Ramvan Museum, Satna 5th- 6th century A.D.

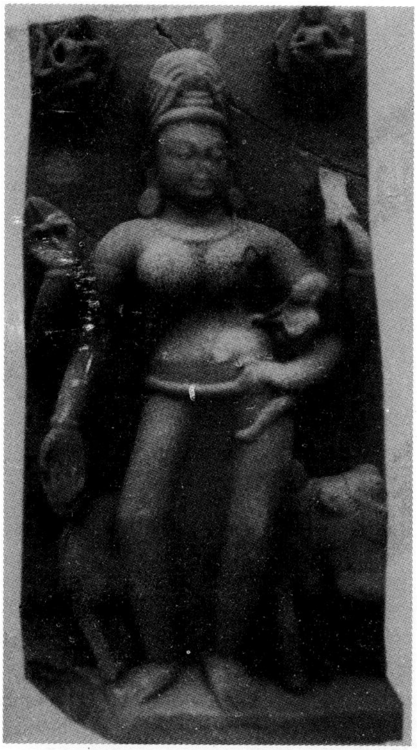

Pl. 12: Maheshwari, Nanchand, Panna (6th century A.D.)

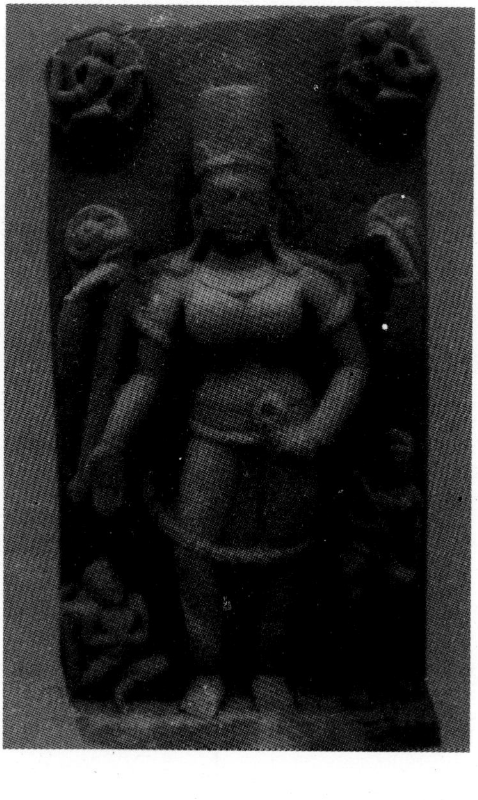

Pl. 13: Vaishnavi, Nanchand, Panna (6th century A.D.)

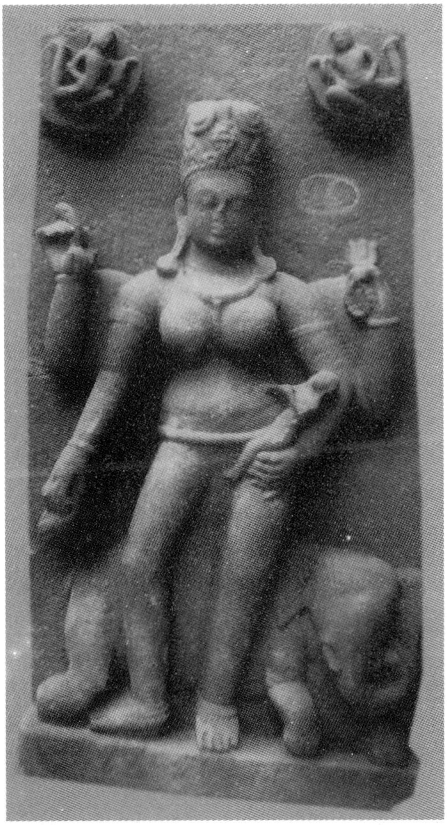

Pl. 14: Indrani,
Nanchand, Panna

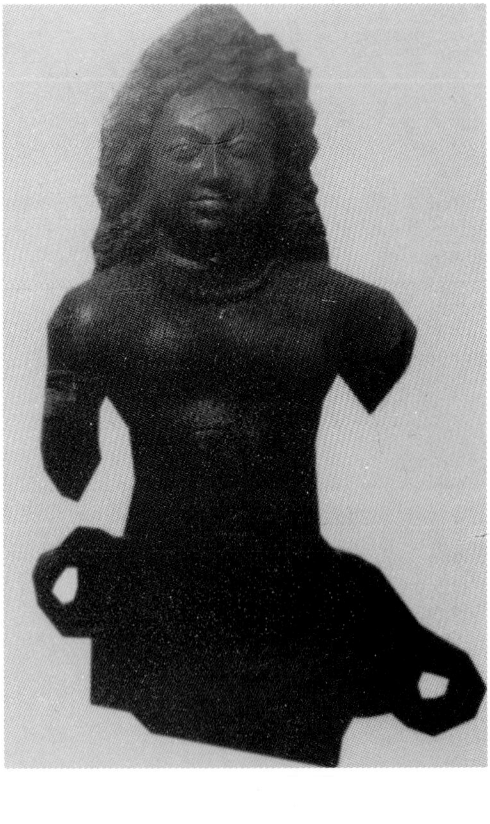

Pl. 15: Divilingi Lakulisha,
Gajendra ghat, Mandsaur
(4th- 5th century A.D.)

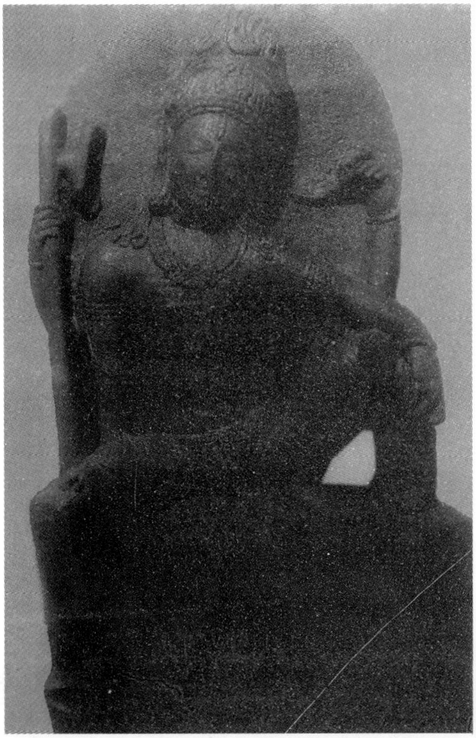

Pl. 16: Siva Lakulisha,
Satna, 5th century A.D.

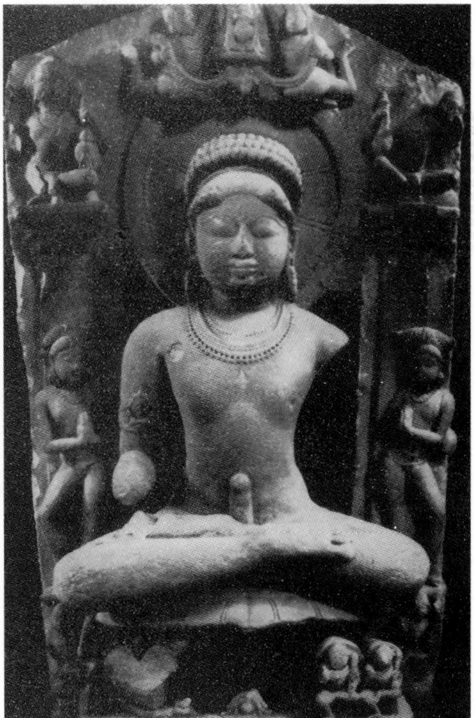

Pl.17: Lakuhsha in
Padmasana Hinglajgarh,
Mandsaur (8th century A.D.)

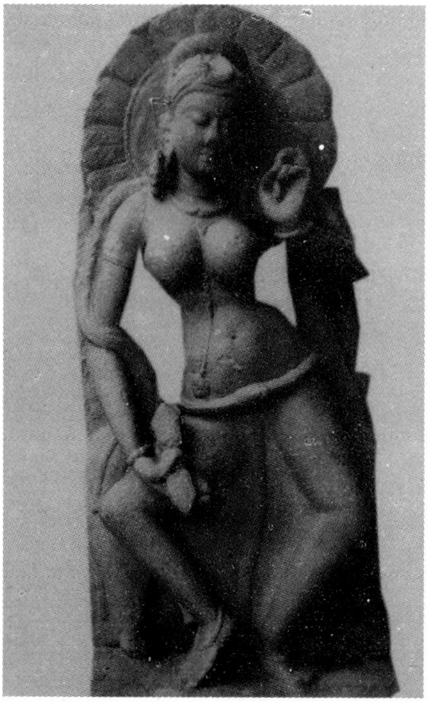

Pl. 18: Indrani, Kota, Shivpuri (7th - 8th century A.D.)

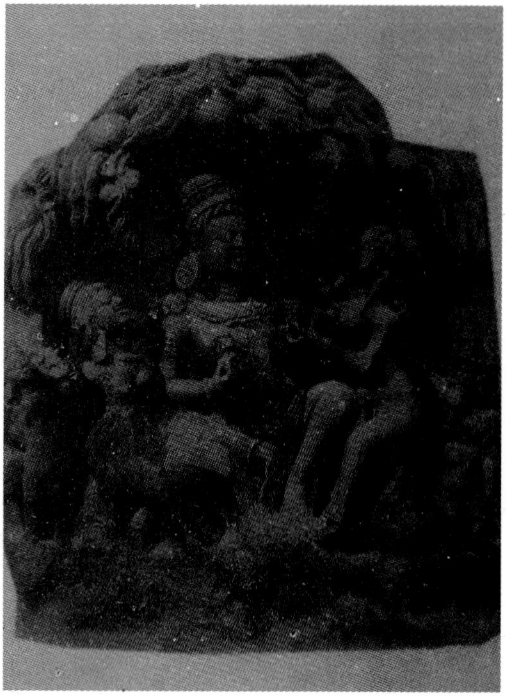

Pl. 19: Kamdeva, Vidisha region, Vidisha (8th century A.D.)

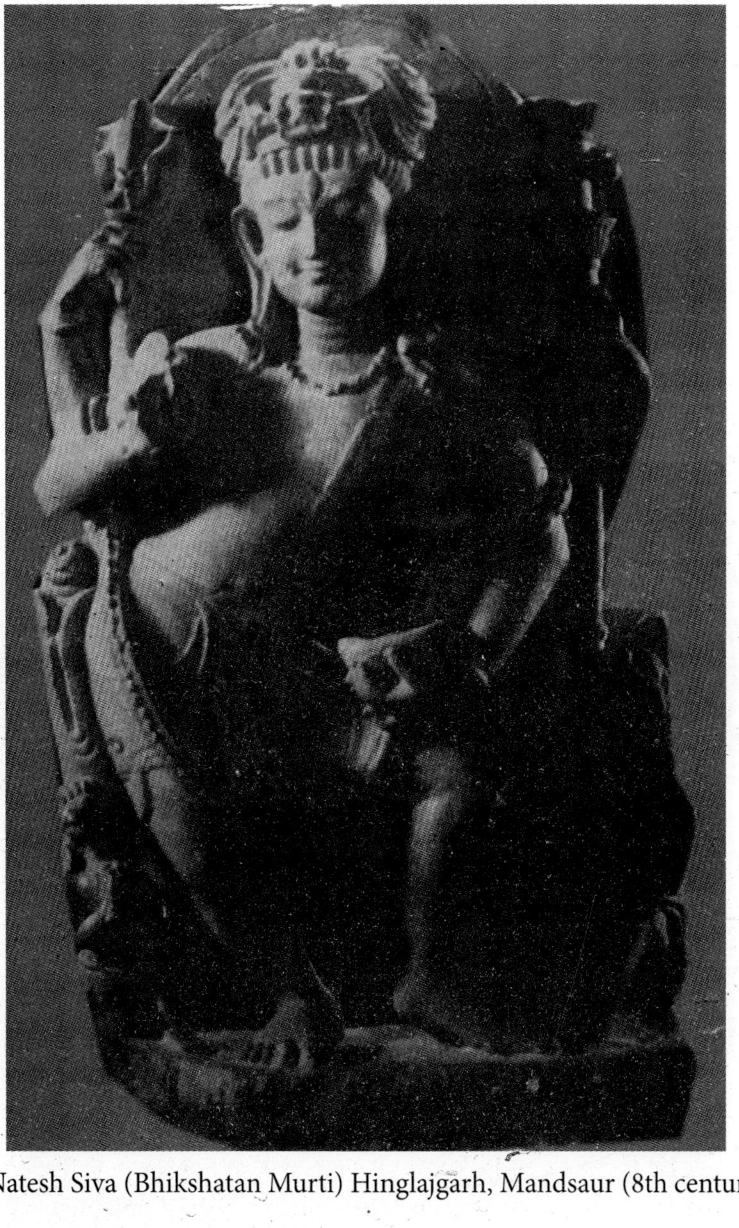

Pl. 20: Natesh Siva (Bhikshatan Murti) Hinglajgarh, Mandsaur (8th century A.D.)

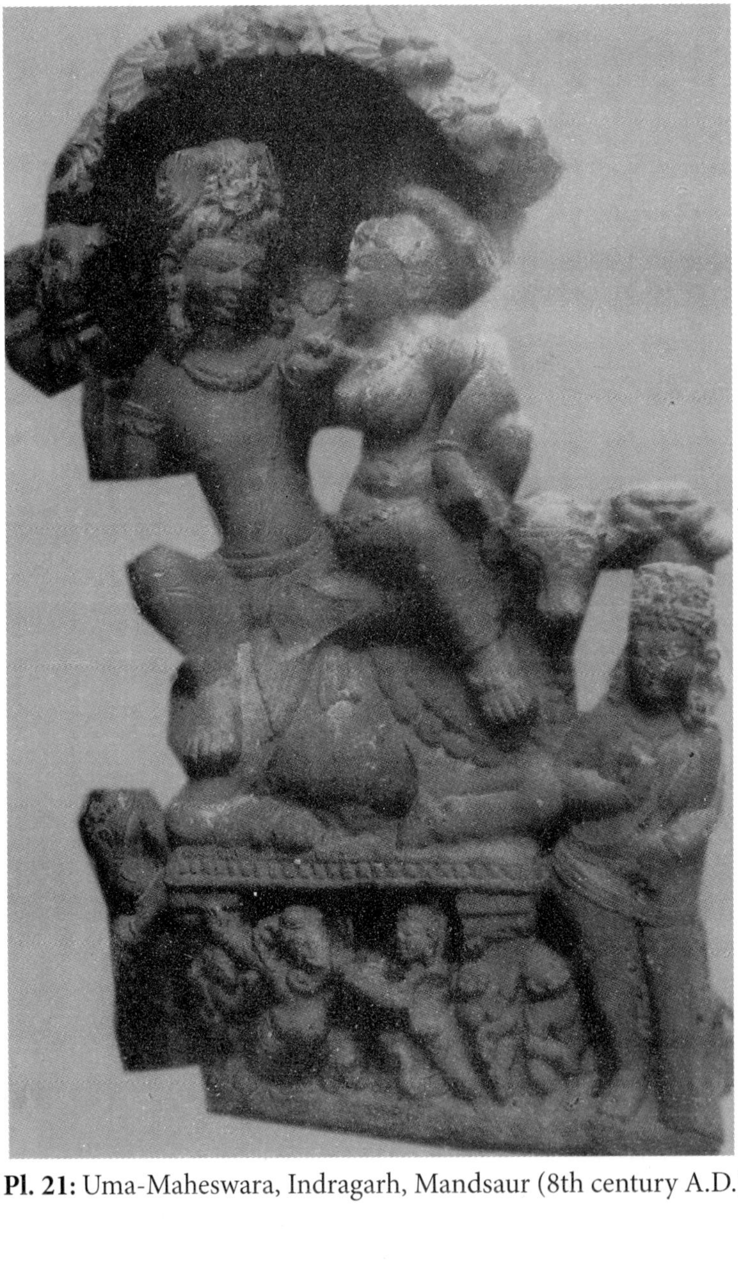

Pl. 21: Uma-Maheswara, Indragarh, Mandsaur (8th century A.D.)

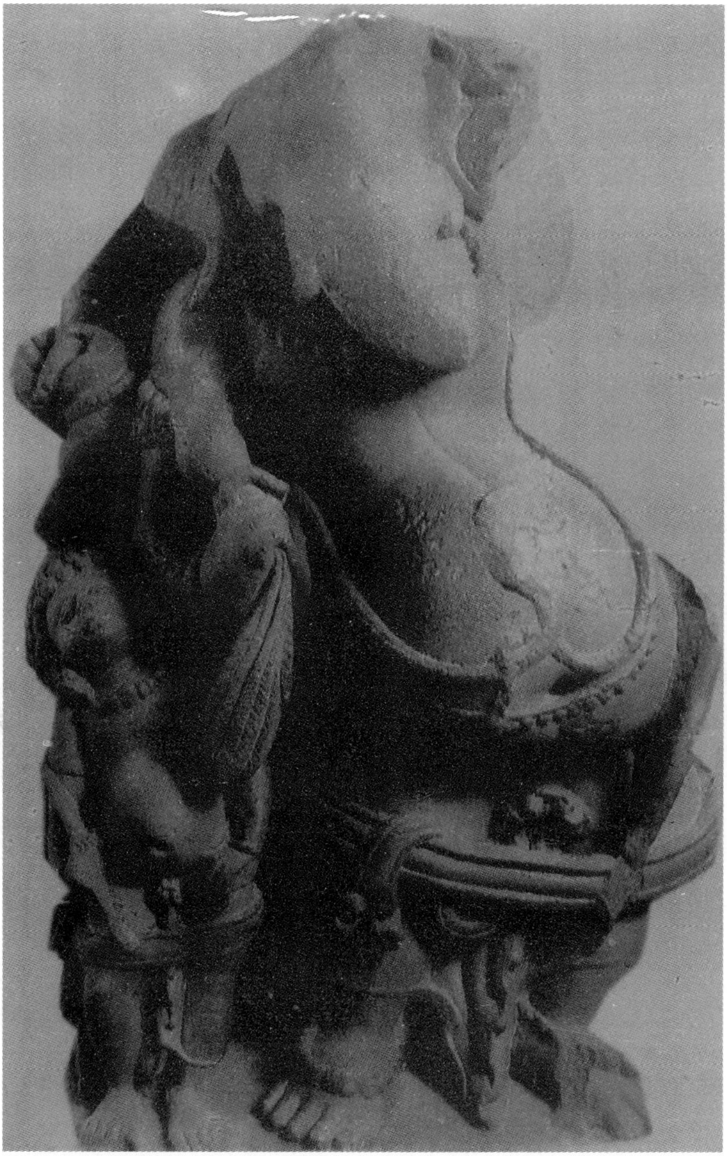

Pl. 22: Ganesh, Keldhar, Shivpuri (8th century A.D.)

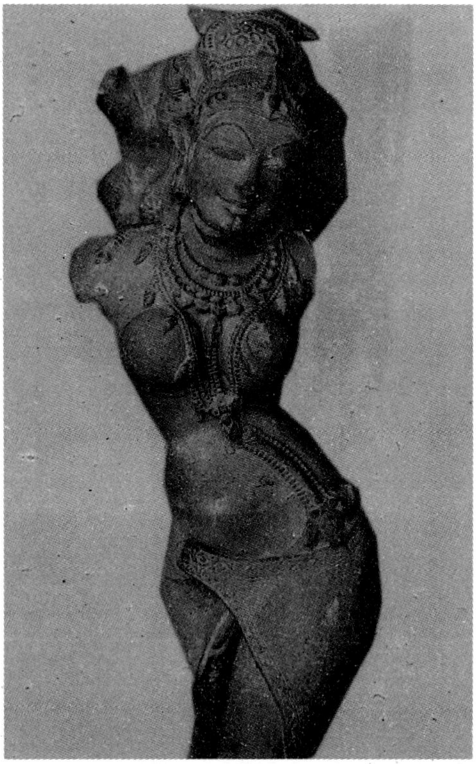

Pl. 23: Shalbhanjika, Gyaraspur, Vidisha (9th - 10th century A.D.)

Pl. 24: Hari- Hara, Shivpuri (Region) Shivpuri (9th - 10th century A.D.)

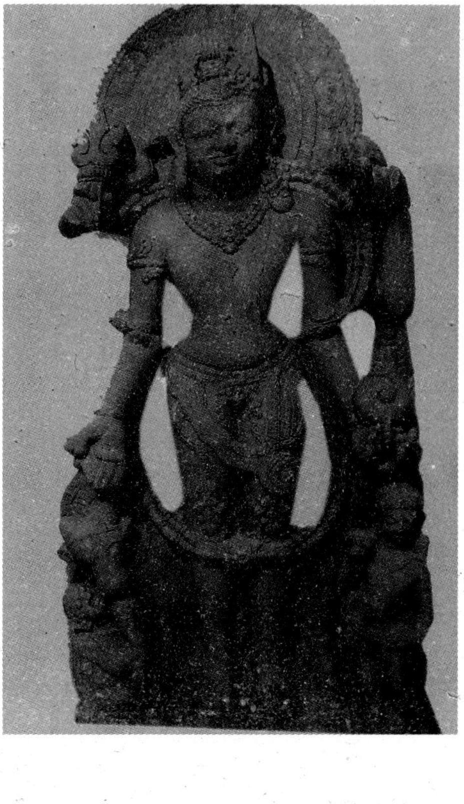

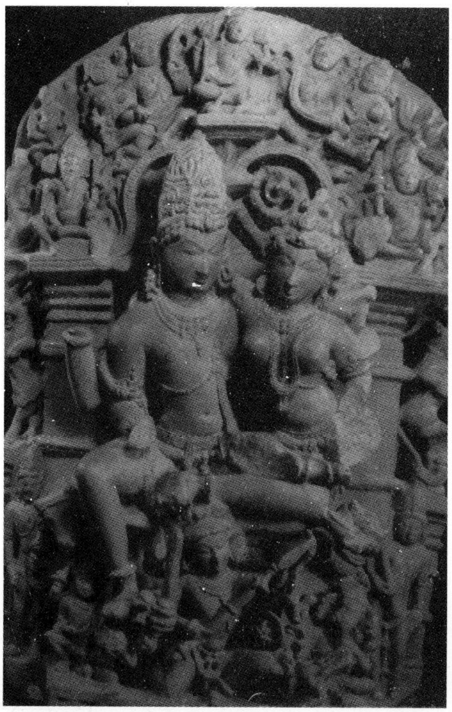

Pl. 25: Uma - Maheswara (Ravananugrha Murti) Hinglajgarh, Mandsaur (11th century A.D.)

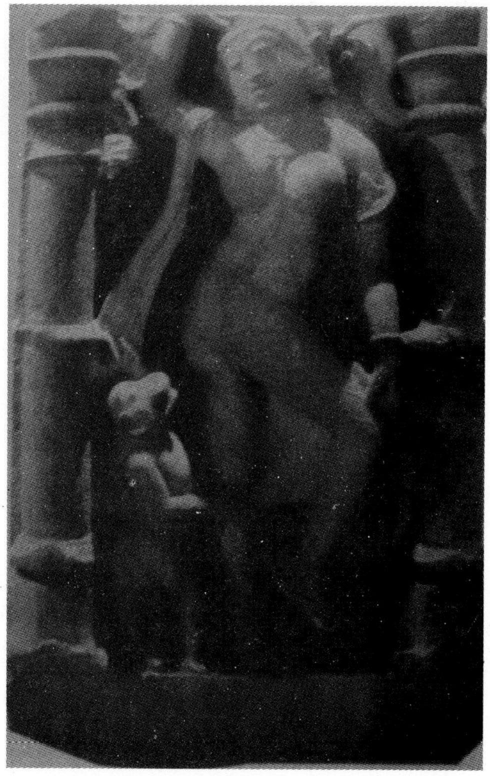

Pl. 26: Abhisarika, Hinglajgarh, Mandsaur (11th century A.D.)

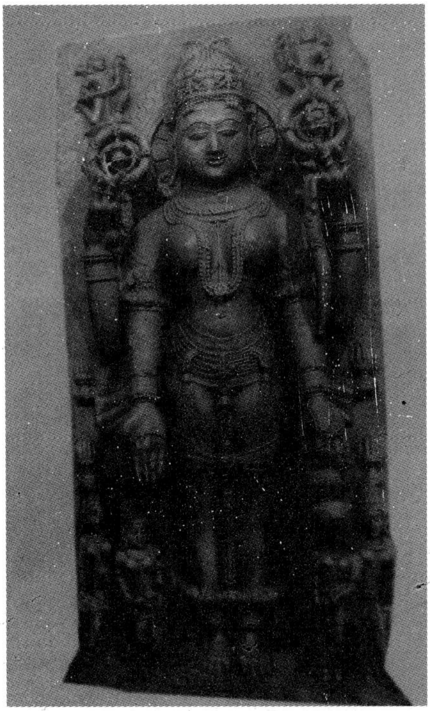

Pl. 27: Gauri, Hinglajgarh, Mandsaur (11th century A.D.)

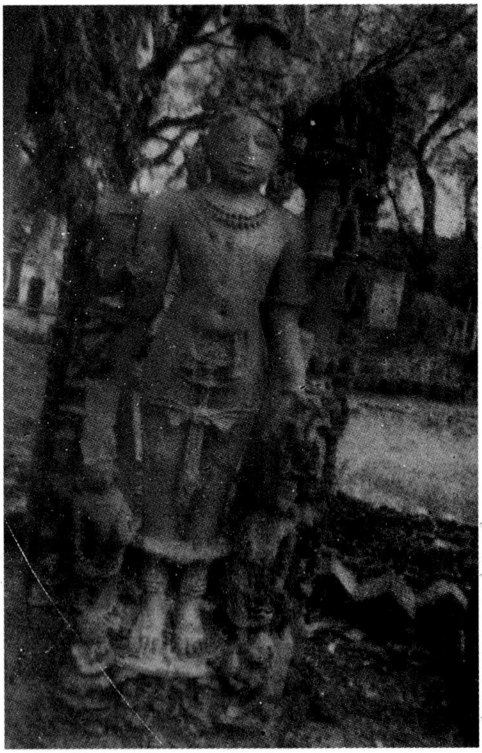

Pl. 28: Visnu (Newly Discovered) Sunari Village, Vidisha (11th century A.D.)

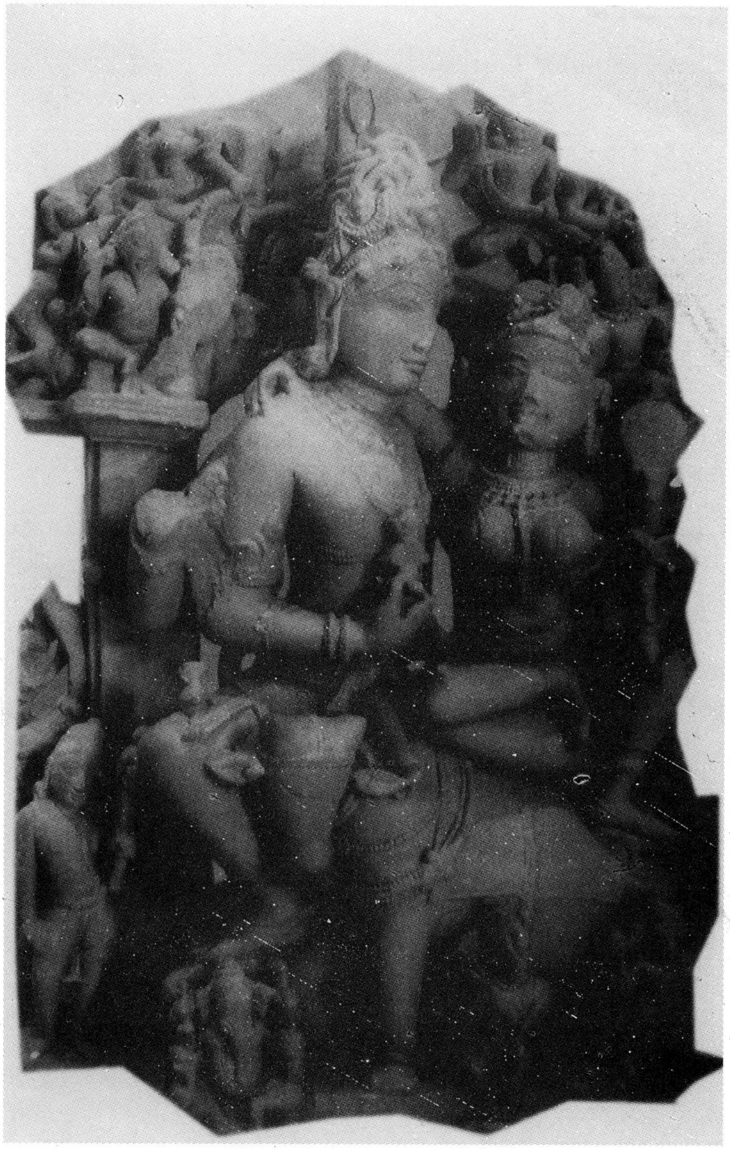

Pl. 29: Uma-Maheswara, Hinglajgarh Mandsaur (11th century A.D.)

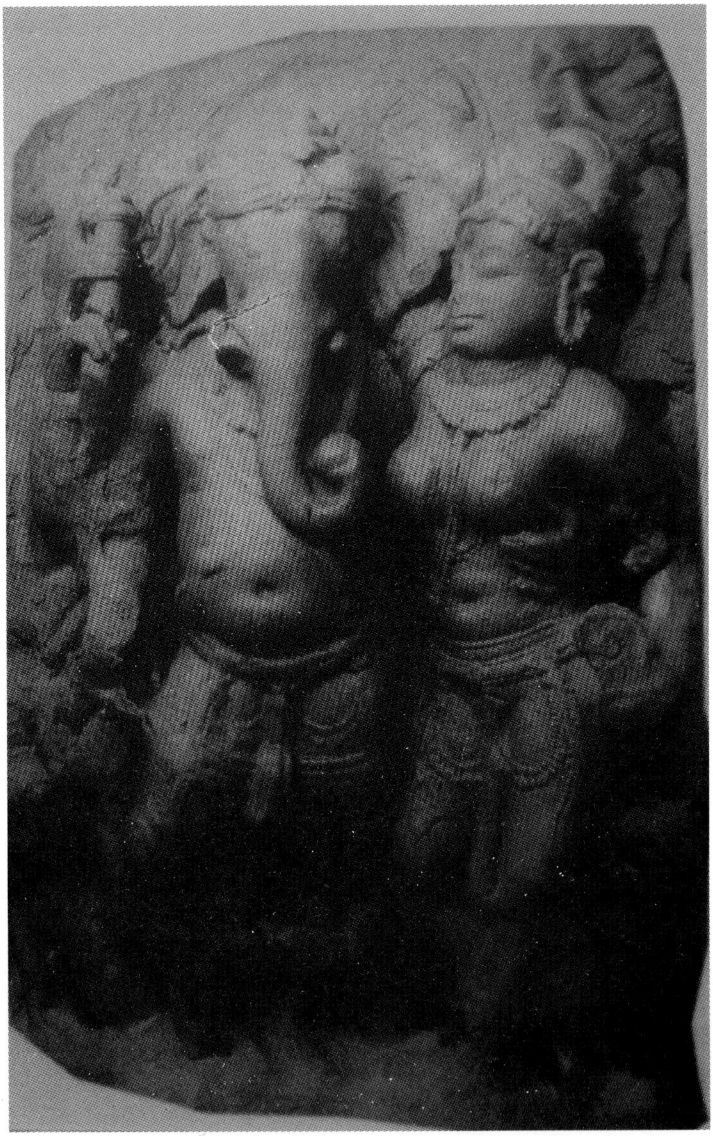

Pl. 30: Shakti Ganesh, Mandsaur (11th century A.D.)

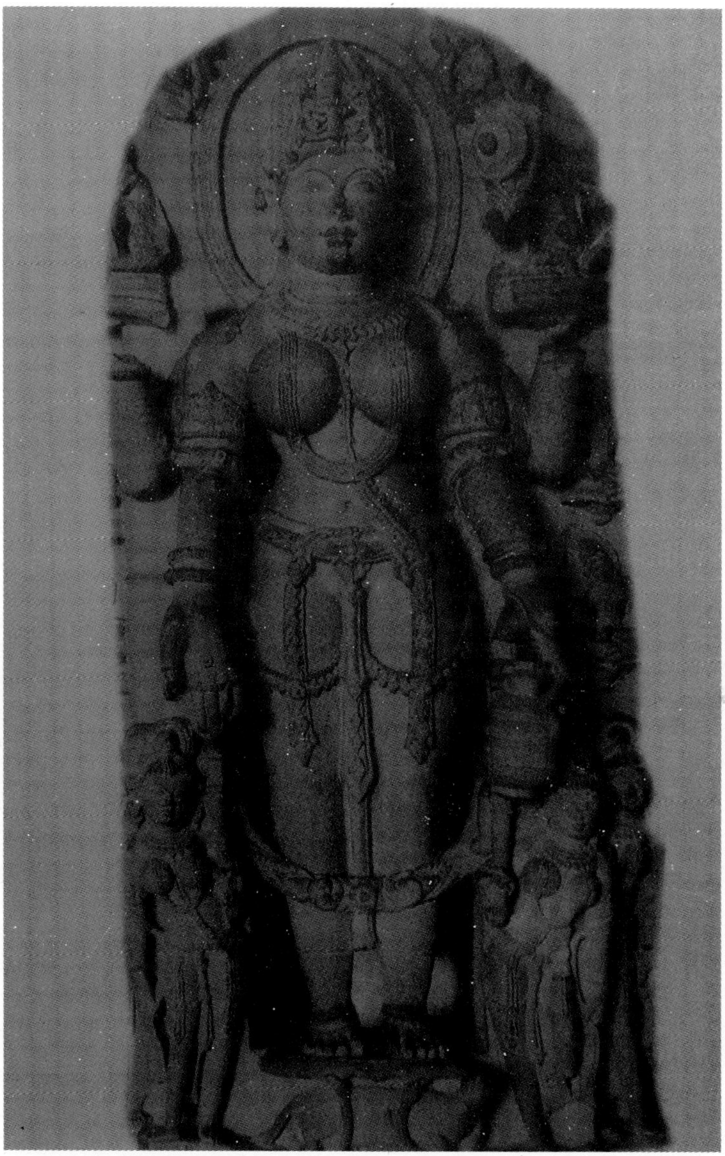

Pl. 31: Parvati, Bhanpura, Mandsaur (11th century A.D.)

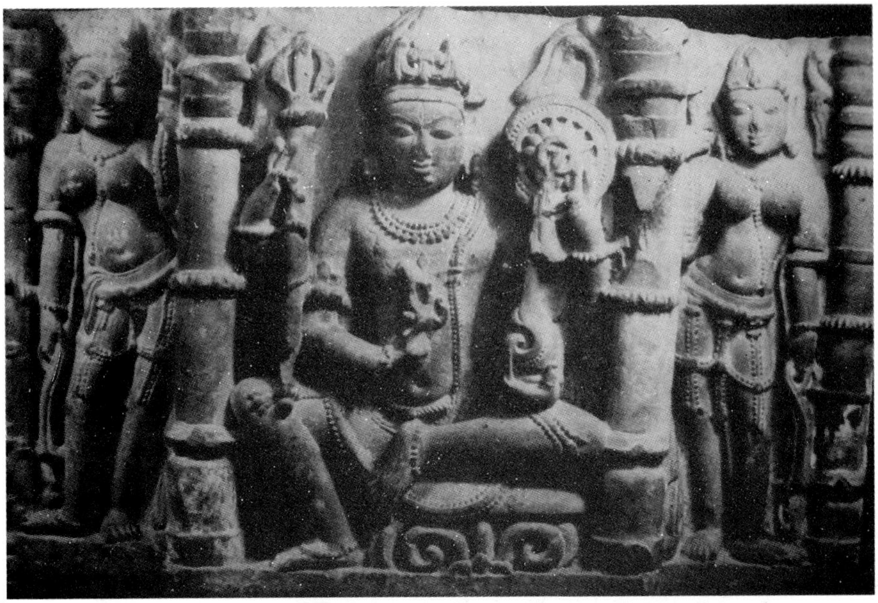

Pl. 32: Hari Hara (Seated in Ardha Padmasana) Hinglajgarh, Mandsaur (11th century A.D.)

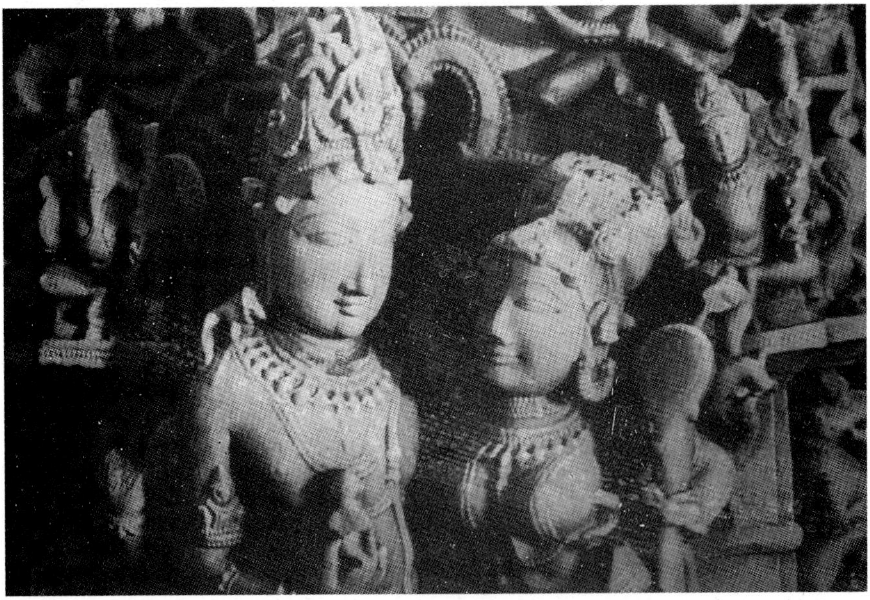

Pl. 33: Uma- Maheswara, Hinglajgarh Mandsaur (11th century A.D.)

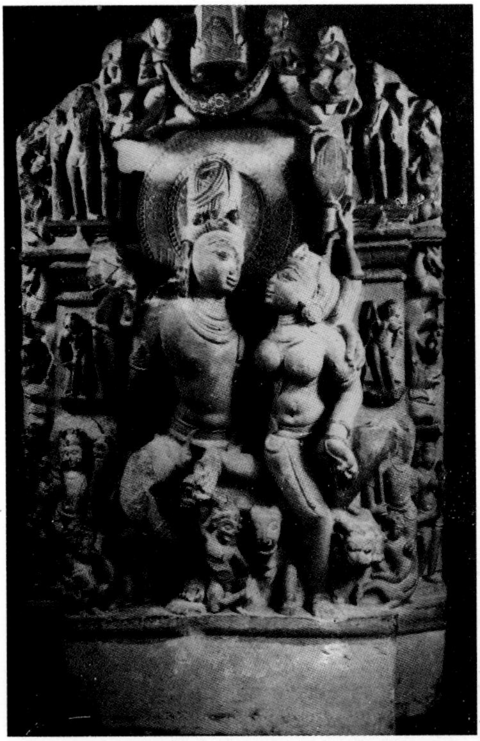

Pl. 34: Uma-Maheswara, Barhad, Bhind (11th century A.D.)

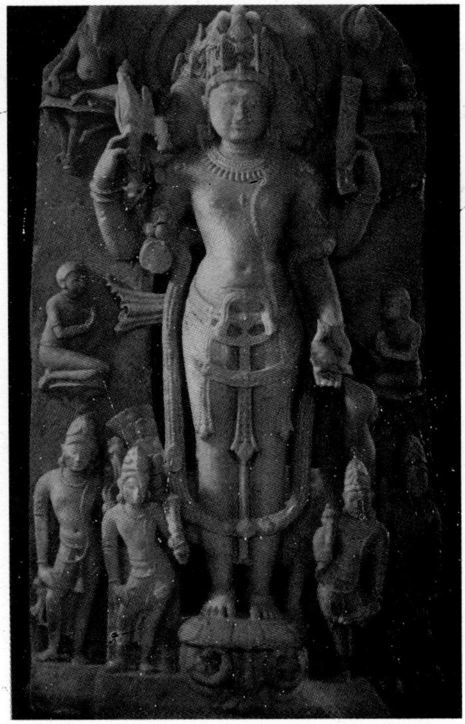

Pl. 35: Kartekeya (Sthanak Murti) Hinglajgarh, Mandsaur (11th century A.D.)

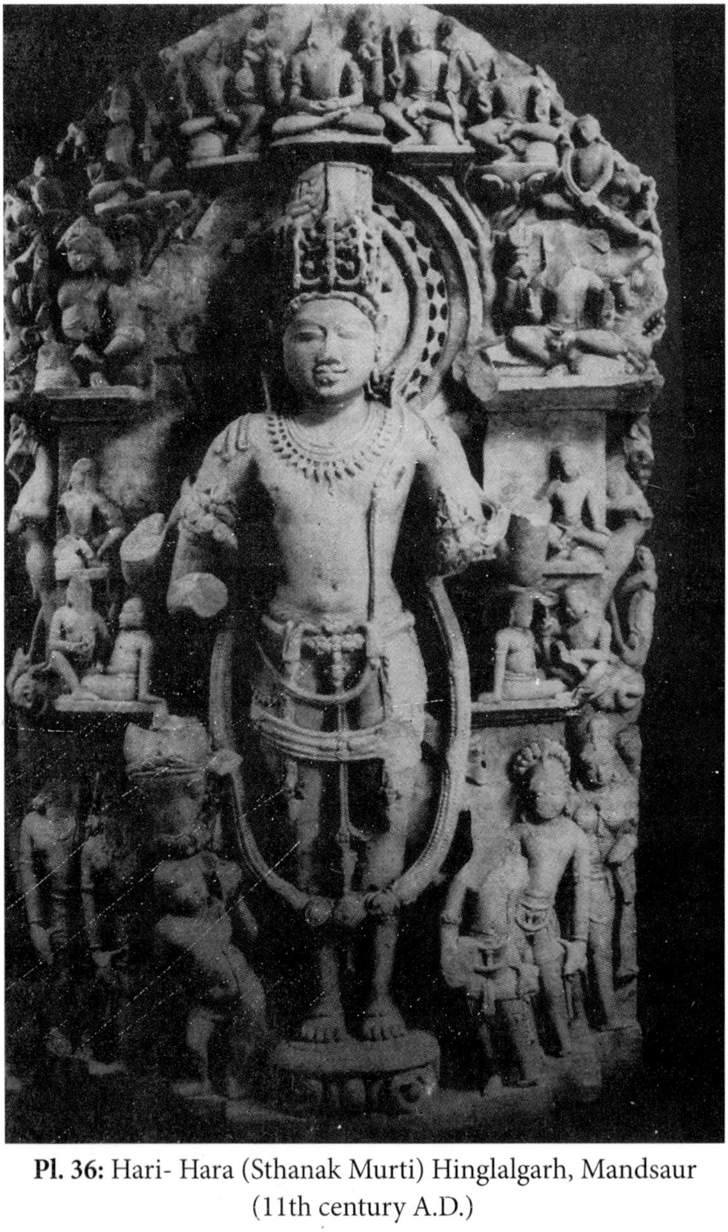

Pl. 36: Hari- Hara (Sthanak Murti) Hinglalgarh, Mandsaur (11th century A.D.)

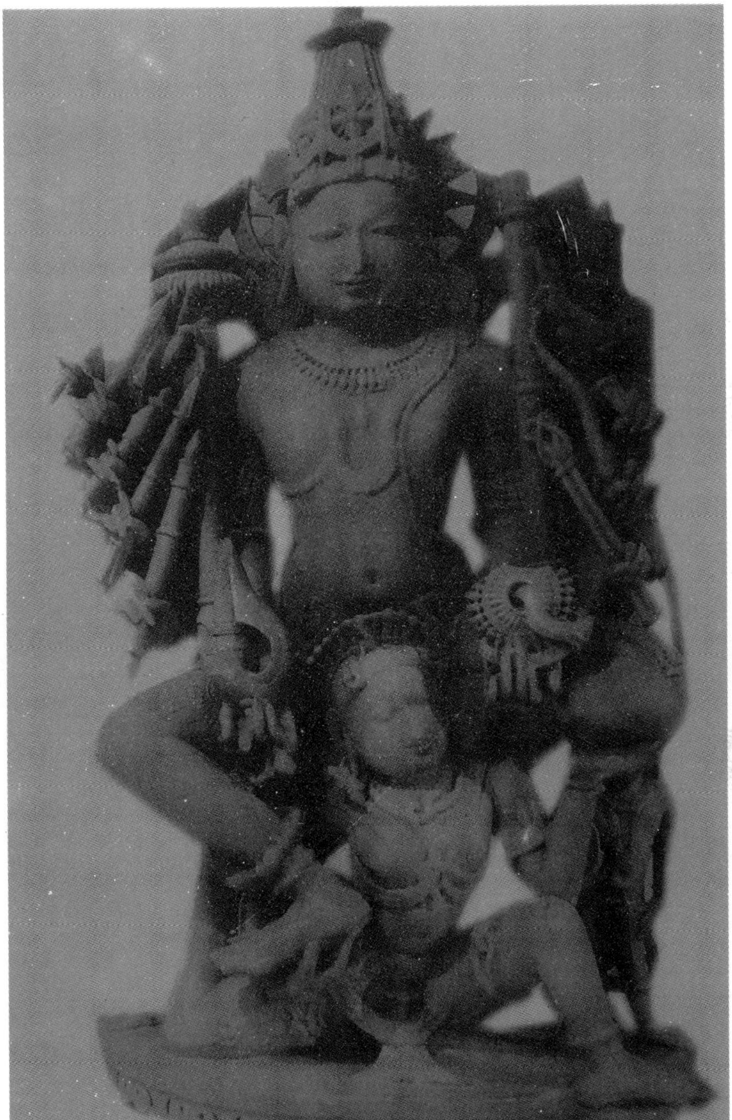

Pl. 37: Visnu, Vidisha (12th century A.D.)

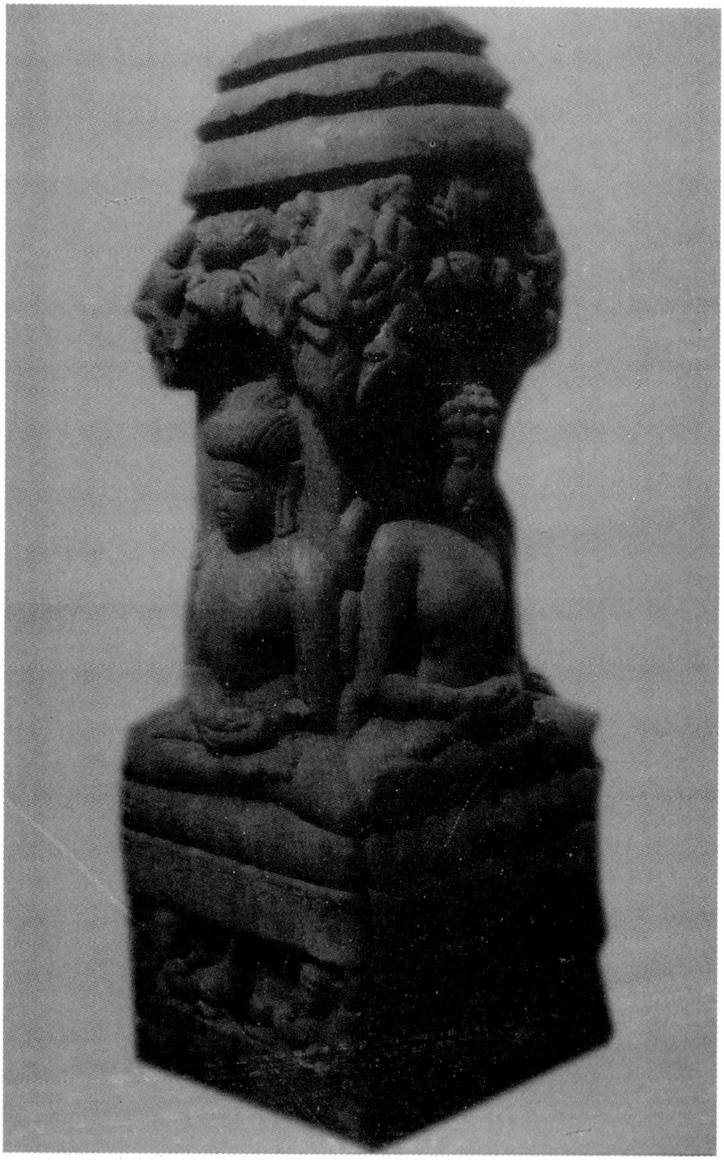

Pl. 38: Jain Chatustika Phulpur, Vidisha (12th century A.D.)

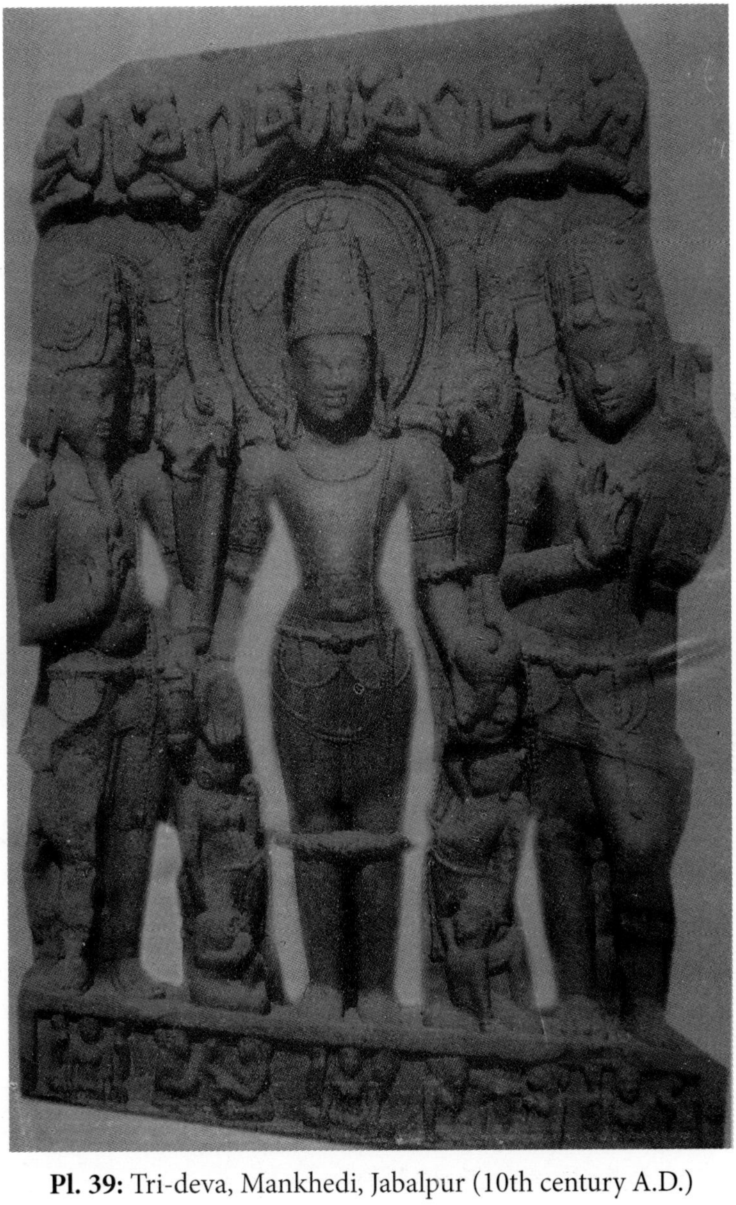

Pl. 39: Tri-deva, Mankhedi, Jabalpur (10th century A.D.)

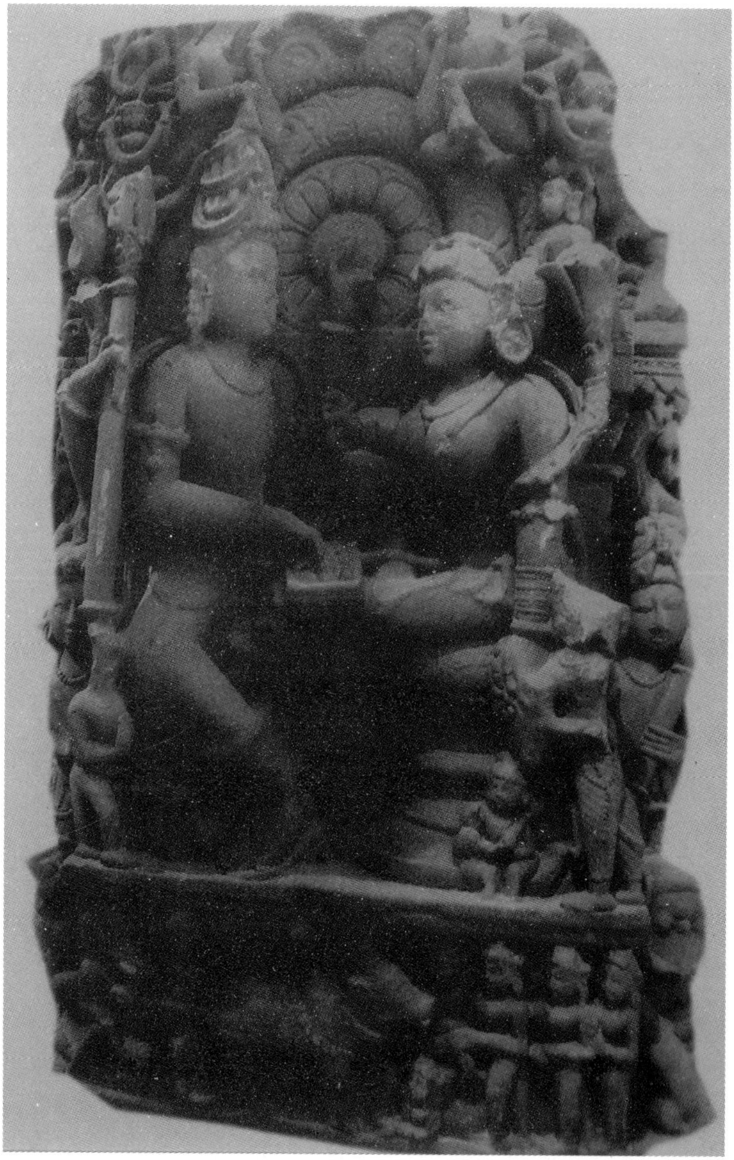

Pl. 40: Uma Maheswara, Jabalpur (10th century A.D.)

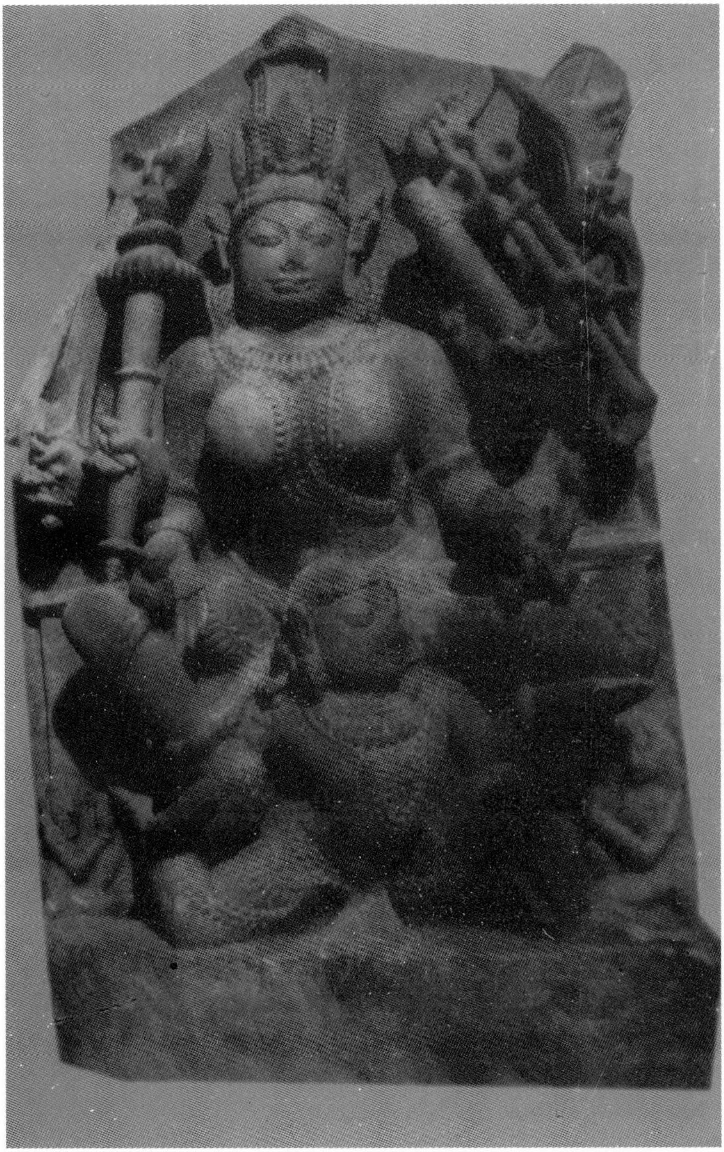

Pl. 41: Vaisnavi, Dhubela, Chhatarpur (11th century A.D.)

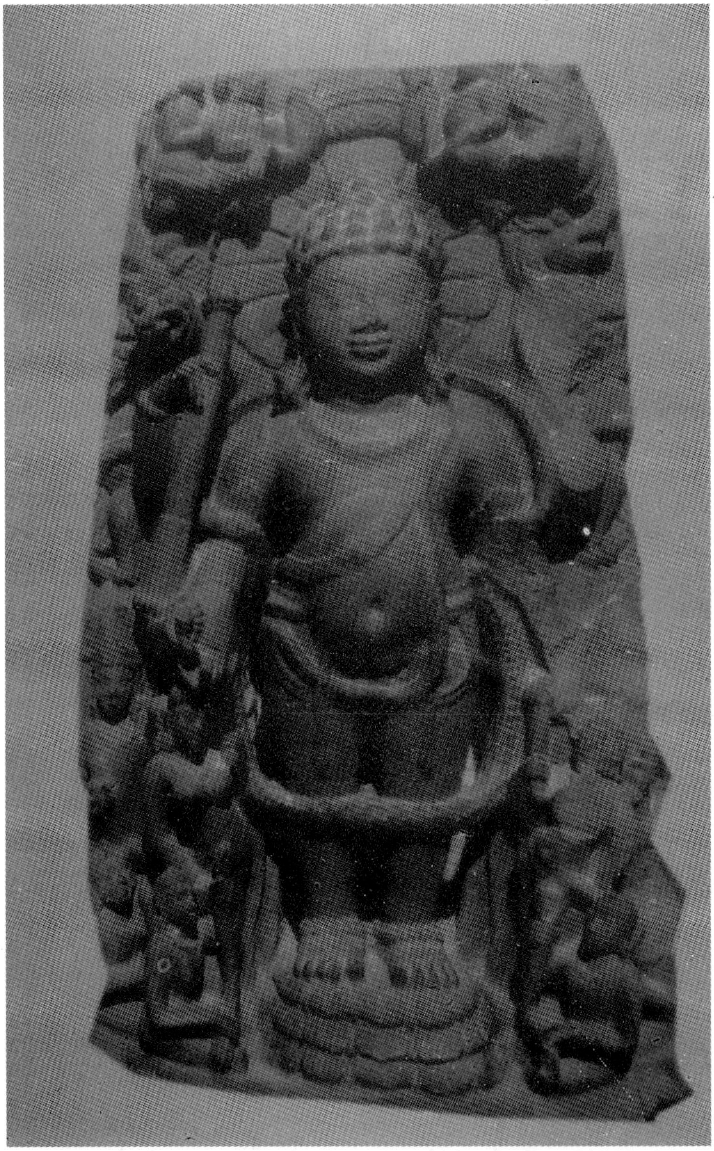

Pl. 42: Vaman, Semaria, Shahdol (11th century A.D.)

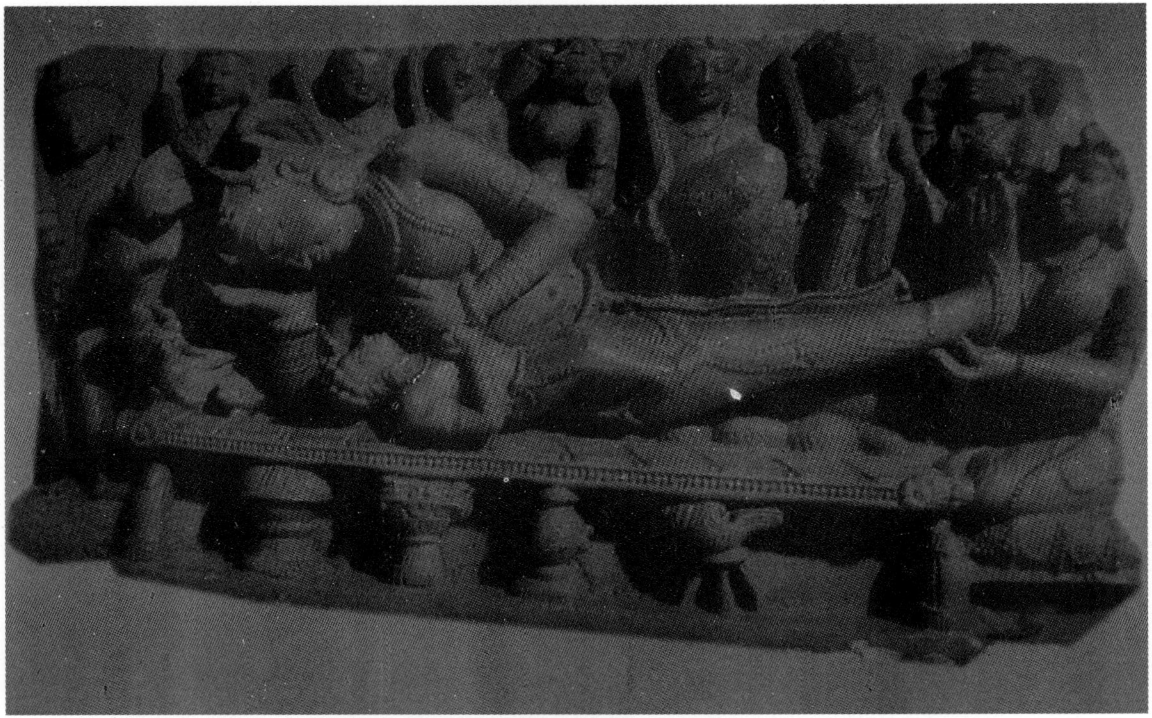

Pl. 43: Krisna- Janma, Shahdol (11th century A.D.)

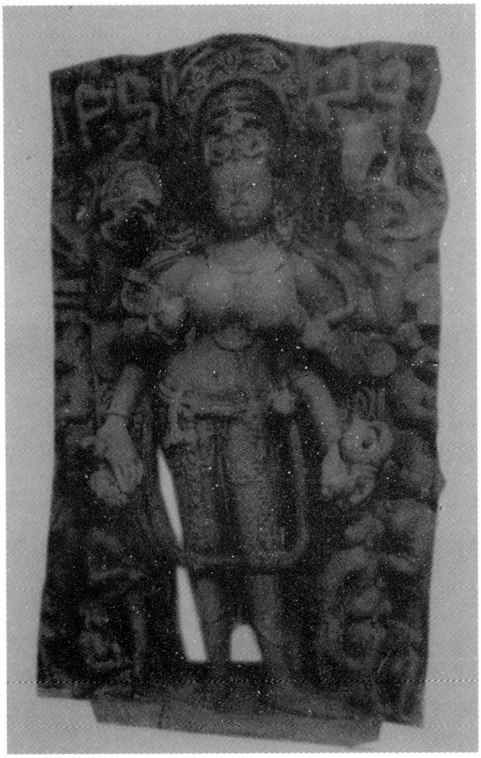

Pl. 44: Yogini Shahdol
(12th century A.D.)

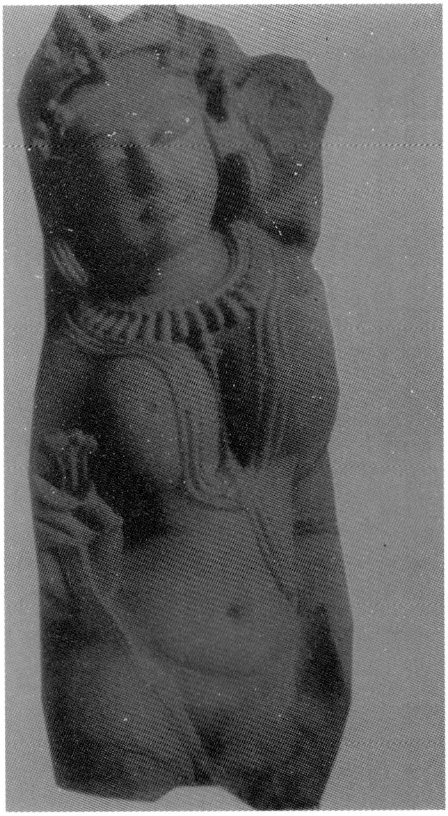

Pl. 45: Skhalit Vasna,
Jabalpur, Museum Jabalpur
(13th century A.D.)

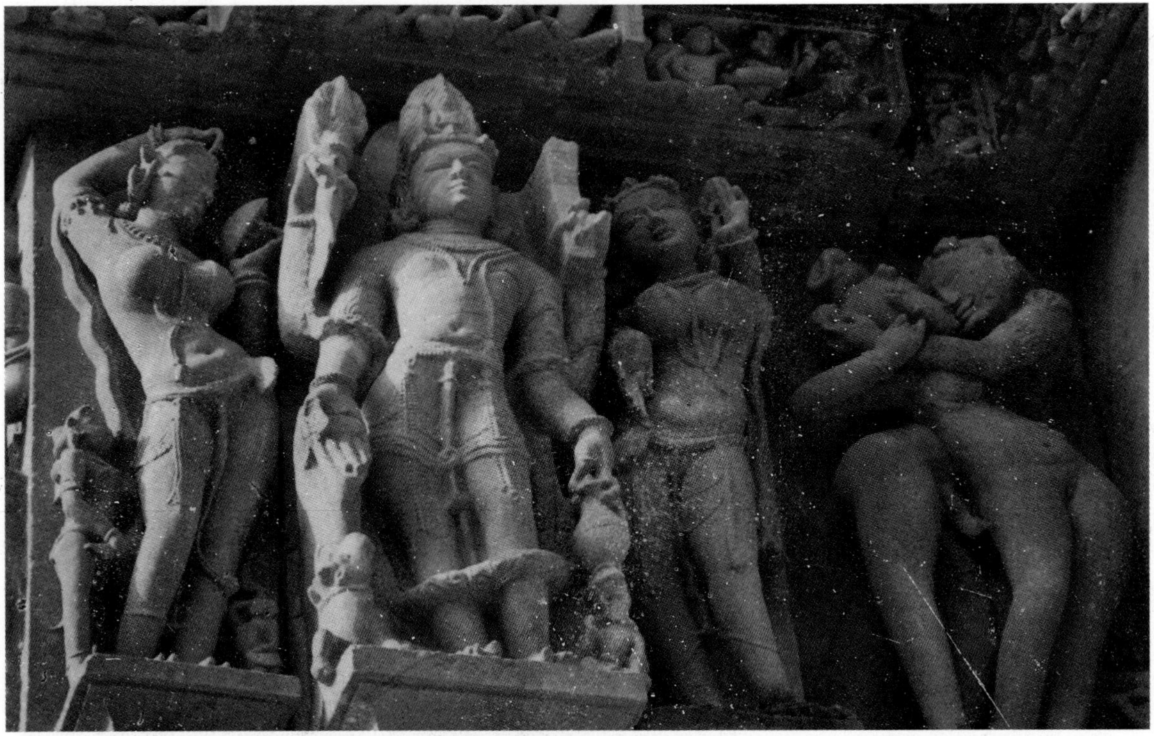

Pl. 46: Siva (Sambhanga) Darpan naika and erotic image (Mithuna Pratima) Khajuraho (Chhatarpur) (10 - 11th century A.D.)

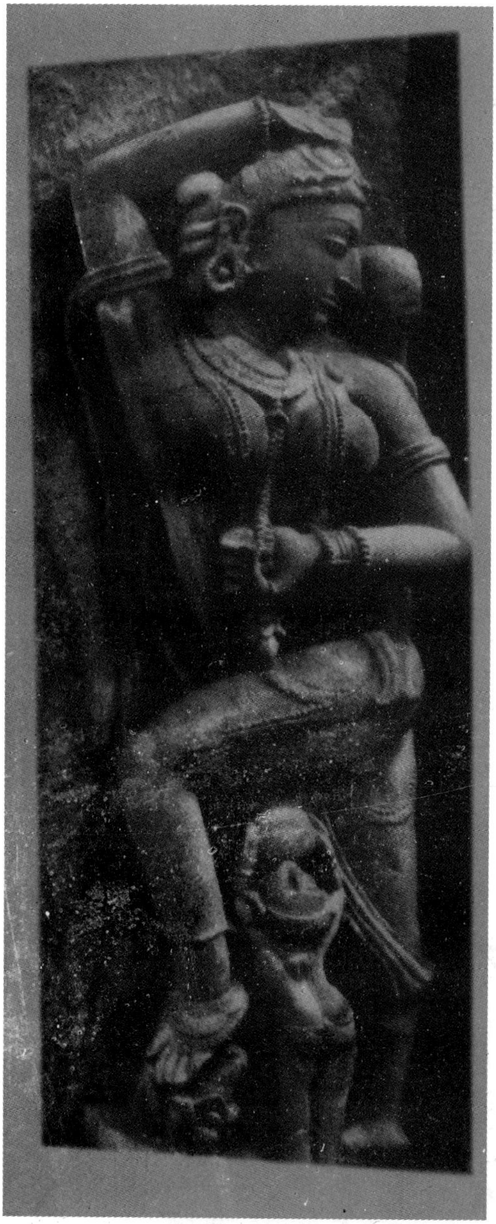

Pl. 47: Apsara, Khajuraho (10 - 11th century A.D.)

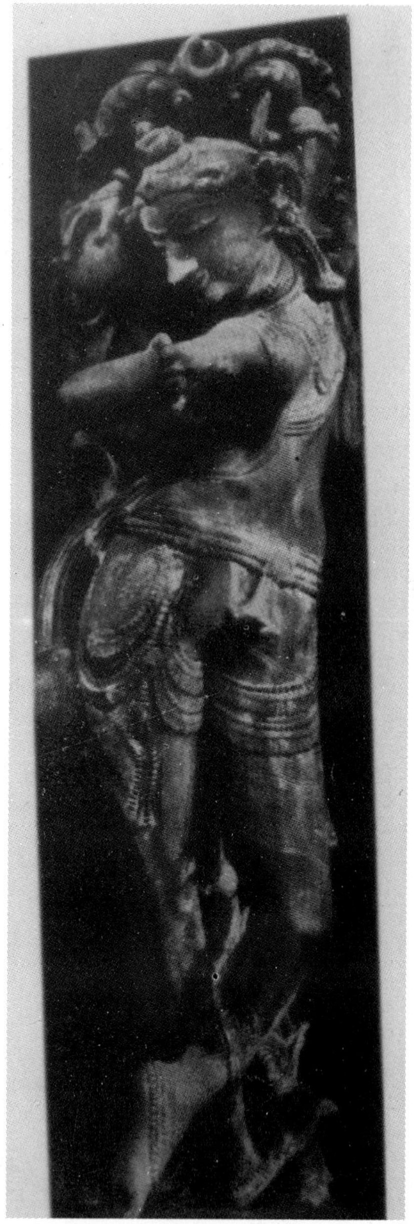

Pl. 48: Apsara, Khajuraho (11th - 12th century A.D.)

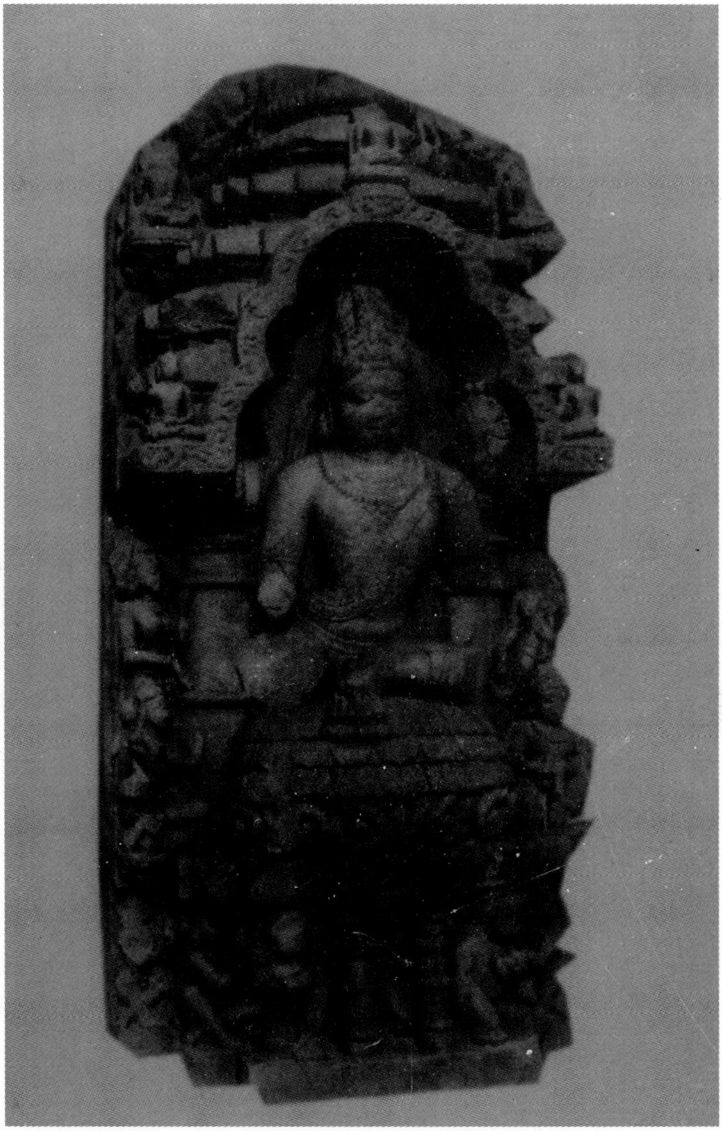

Pl. 49: Avlokites'wara, Mausania, Chhatarpur (10th century A.D.)

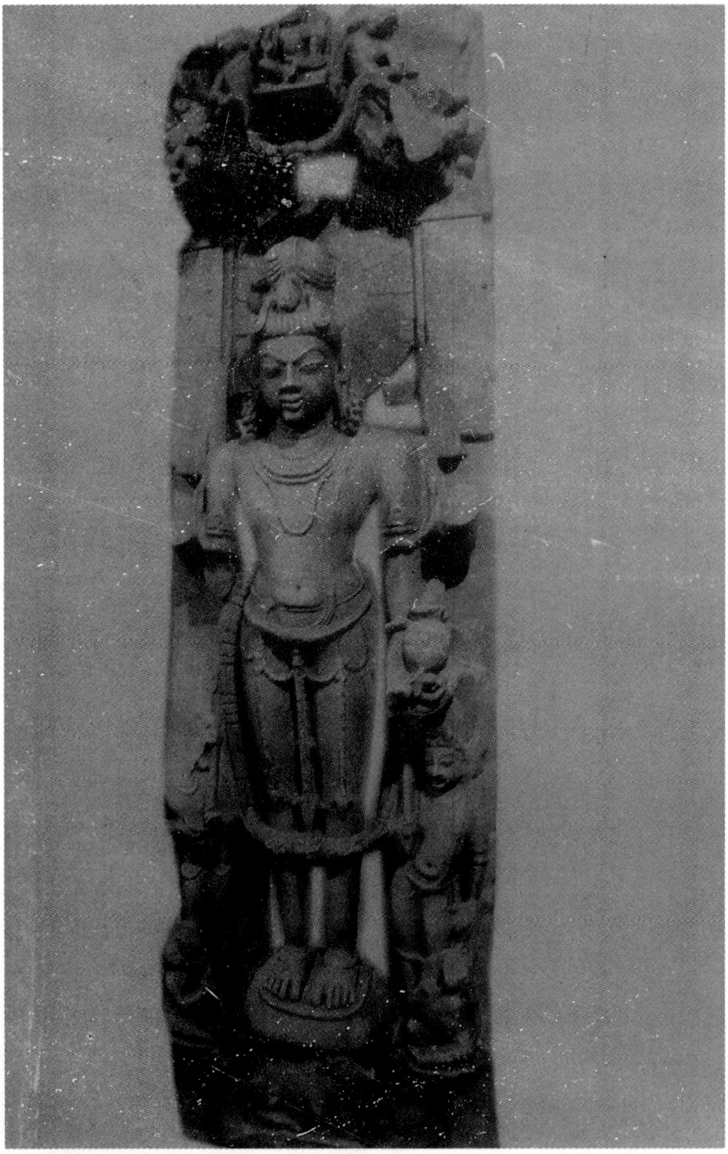

Pl. 50: Siva Barhad, Bhind (11th century A.D.)

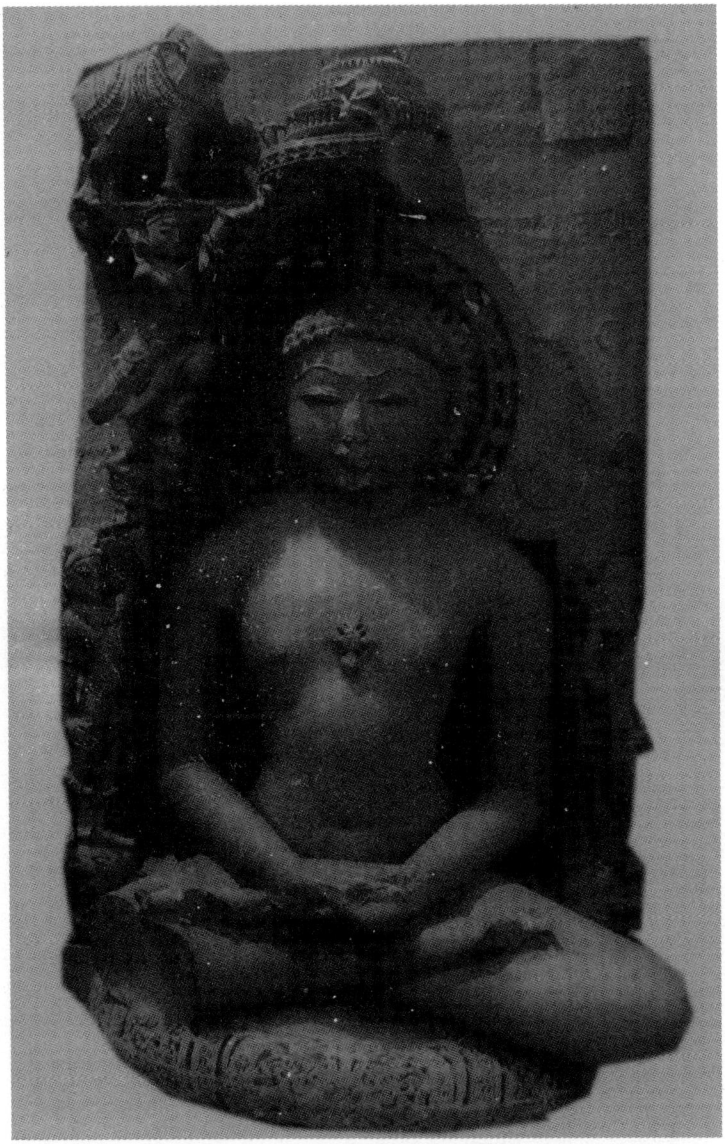

Pl. 51: Adinath Narwar, Shivpuri (12th century A.D.)

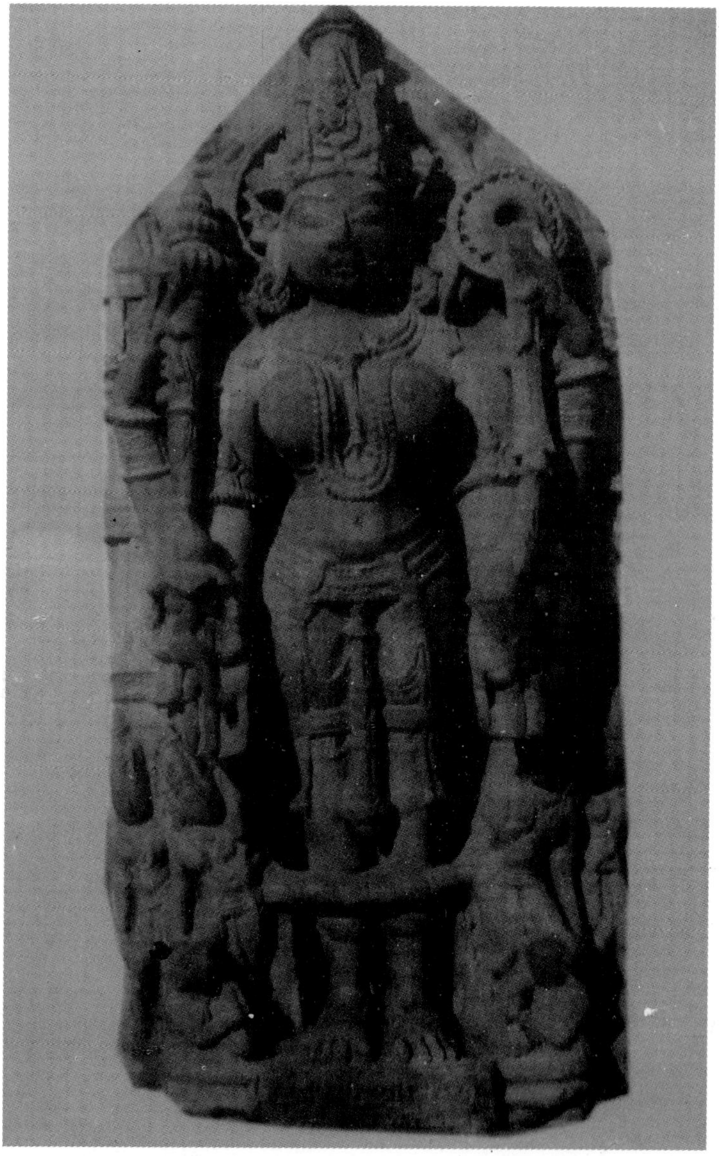

Pl. 52: Vaisnavi, Shivpuri (11 - 12th century A.D.)

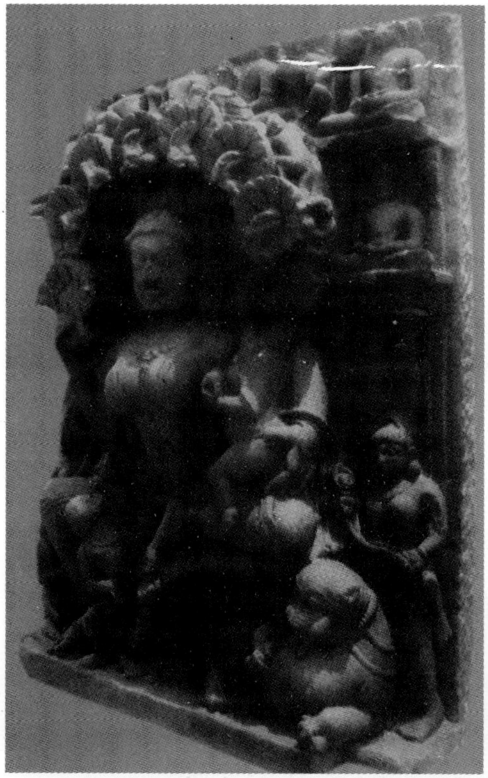

Pl. 53: Ambika, Shivpuri (11th - 12th century A.D.)

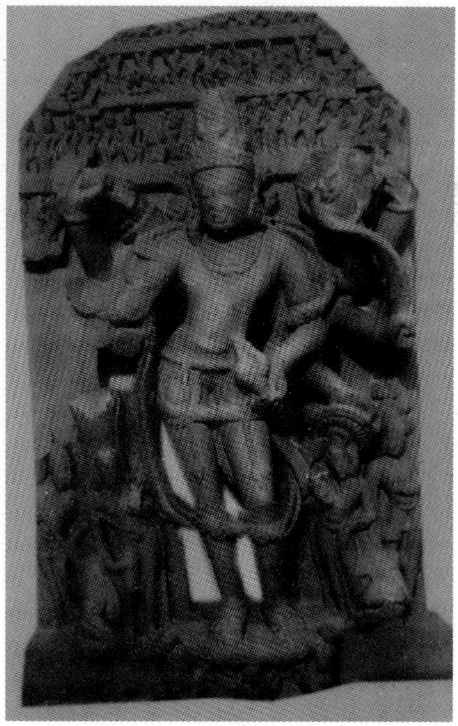

Pl. 54: Visnu, Vishvarupa, Suhania, Morena (10th century A.D.)

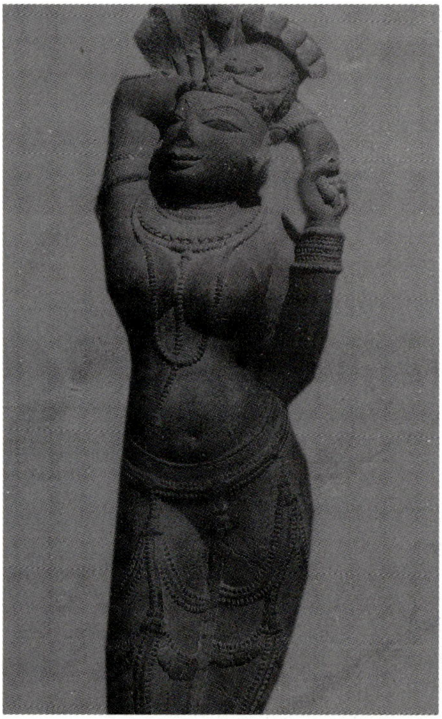

Pl. 55: Alas Naika Morena
(10th century A.D.)

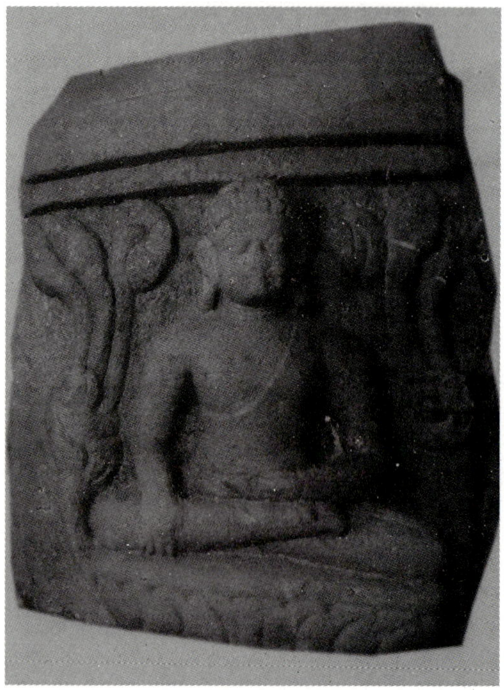

Pl. 56: Buddha (Seated in Padmasana) (Bhumisparsa mudra) Keldhar, Shivpuri (10th century A.D.)